# STRANGE TALES
# OF WORLD TRAVEL

# A SELECTION OF TRAVELERS' TALES BOOKS

### Country and Regional Guides
30 Days in Italy, 30 Days in the South Pacific, America, Antarctica, Australia, Brazil, Central America, China, Cuba, France, Greece, India, Ireland, Italy, Japan, Mexico, Nepal, Spain, Thailand, Tibet, Turkey; Alaska, American Southwest, Grand Canyon, Hawai'i, Hong Kong, Middle East, Paris, Prague, Provence, San Francisco, South Pacific, Tuscany

### Women's Travel
100 Places Every Woman Should Go, 100 Places in Italy Every Woman Should Go, 100 Places in France Every Woman Should Go, 100 Places in Greece Every Woman Should Go, 100 Places in the USA Every Woman Should Go, 100 Places in Cuba Every Woman Should Go, 50 Places in Rome, Florence, & Venice Every Woman Should Go, Best Women's Travel Writing, Gutsy Women, Mother's World, Safety and Security for Women Who Travel, Wild with Child, Woman's Asia, Woman's Europe, Woman's Path, Woman's World, Woman's World Again, Women in the Wild

### Body & Soul
Food, How to Eat Around the World, A Mile in Her Boots, Pilgrimage, Road Within

### Special Interest
Danger!, Gift of Birds, Gift of Rivers, Gift of Travel, How to Shit Around the World, Hyenas Laughed at Me, Leave the Lipstick, Take the Iguana, More Sand in My Bra, Mousejunkies!, Not So Funny When It Happened, Sand in My Bra, Testosterone Planet, There's No Toilet Paper on the Road Less Traveled, Thong Also Rises, What Color Is your Jockstrap?, Wake Up and Smell the Shit, The World Is a Kitchen, Writing Away, China Option, La Dolce Vita U

### Travel Literature
The Best Travel Writing, Soul of a Great Traveler, Deer Hunting in Paris, Fire Never Dies, Ghost Dance in Berlin, Guidebook Experiment, Kin to the Wind, Kite Strings of the Southern Cross, Last Trout in Venice, Marco Polo Didn't Go There, Rivers Ran East, Royal Road to Romance, A Sense of Place, Shopping for Buddhas, Soul of Place, Storm, Sword of Heaven, Take Me With You, Unbeaten Tracks in Japan, Way of Wanderlust, Wings, Coast to Coast, Mother Tongue, Baboons for Lunch

# STRANGE TALES OF WORLD TRAVEL

## BIZARRE, MYSTERIOUS, HORRIBLE, HILARIOUS

### GINA & SCOTT GAILLE

TRAVELERS' TALES,
AN IMPRINT OF SOLAS HOUSE, INC.
PALO ALTO

Travelers' Tales and Solas House are trademarks of Solas House, Inc., Palo Alto, California. travelerstales.com | solashouse.com

Art Direction: Kimberly Nelson
Cover Design: Kimberly Nelson
Interior Design and Page Layout: Howie Severson/Fortuitous Publishing

Photo Credits:
Chapters 7, 10-11, 15, 21, 25-27, 31, 36, 41, 43-44, 47, and 49-50 (Gina & Scott Gaille)
Chapter 9 (Ariyo Olasunkanmi/Shutterstock.com)
Chapter 12 (EQ Roy/Shutterstock.com)
Chapter 13 (Bumihills/Shutterstock.com)
Chapter 17 (Art Konovalov/Shutterstock.com)
Chapter 19 (An Aussie Airliners Copyright Image)
Chapter 20 (WJR Visuals/Shutterstock.com)
Chapter 32 (La Zona/Shutterstock.com)
Chapter 35 (Brian Kimball/Wikimedia Commons)
Chapter 39 (Amophoto_au/Shutterstock.com)
Chapter 45 (Xuanhuongho/Shutterstock.com)
Chapter 46 (Chameleons Eye/Shuttersock.com)
Chapter 48 (Gary Roberts/Alamy Stock Photo)
Others (Shutterstock.com)

Library of Congress Cataloging-in-Publication Data is available upon request

978-1-60952-169-1 (paperback)
978-1-60952-170-7 (ebook)
978-1-60952-171-4 (hard cover)

First Edition
Printed in the United States
10 9 8 7 6 5 4 3 2 1

*To all those who have been kind enough
to share their stories with us*

# Author's Note

This book is a memoir. It reflects our current recollections of our experiences over time and the stories we have heard. Some names and details have been changed, some events have been compressed, and some dialogue has been recreated. We also would like to thank the many people we have met on our travels for being generous enough to share their stories with us. We recognize that their memories of the events described in this book may be different from those of others who experienced them. The tales in this book were represented to us as being factual. Whether entirely true or not, each story conveys meaning about a place, how someone has experienced it, and how we remembered it.

# Table of Contents

# Foreword

*Our Infinitely Surprising World*

DON GEORGE

~

"What's the strangest thing you have ever experienced or seen?"

This simple question beats at the heart of this extraordinary collection.

For more than two decades, Scott Gaille's work as an international corporate lawyer has taken him to the farthest corners of the globe. Rather than fly home as soon as business is done, he has used these assignments to explore local countries and cultures, frequently accompanied by his wife and partner in wanderlust, Gina.

Through these explorations, they have met an astonishing variety of people. Fueled by a deep curiosity about human nature and an appetite for adventure, they have asked these people that simple question: "What's the strangest thing you have ever experienced or seen?" Then they have listened—and amazing tales have unfolded.

This book collects 50 of those tales.

The storytellers range richly in geography and social stratum: from a Mauritanian diplomat and an Omani government minister to an Icelandic farmer and a Tanzanian miner, a British secret service agent to a masseur in Madagascar to a Galápagos wildlife naturalist. They include an Australian road kill artist, an

American oil executive, a South African big game guide, the first Hmong lawyer in Laos, the English "fourth girlfriend" of a Russian tycoon, and dozens more.

As this marvelously motley cast of storytellers suggests, *Strange Tales of World Travel* presents a world you will not find in glossy magazine articles, breathless blogs, or self-adulatory Instagrams. Instead, it's a world of adventures gone awry with gorillas, Cape buffalos, tiger snakes, and other wildlife, of rare Vodun and Mayan rituals, of intimate glimpses of unimaginable wealth and unquestionable power, of close encounters with the wilder edges of human culture, including Ebola, shrunken heads, and ancient shamanistic rites.

The result is a collection that is, as the book's subtitle suggests, bizarre, mysterious, horrible, and hilarious—like travel, and life, itself.

When Gina and Scott approached me about working with them to assemble a collection of their travel tales, my initial reaction was extreme hesitation. Over 40 years as a travel writer and editor, I've met dozens of people who have wandered fervently to far-flung places, penned detailed journals, dispatched epic emails, and become convinced that their accounts were destined to become bestsellers. Great travel writing, of course, requires more than outlandish adventures in exotic places, and I was worried that Gina and Scott might turn out to be two more members of this tribe of travelers whose worldly passions far surpass their wordly talents.

Then they sent me a sampling of their tales—and I was hooked.

From their first story, a sea-guide's account of a seemingly hapless (but ultimately charmed) tourist's encounter with a predatory shark, the Gailles' tales charted a territory that was delightfully different from the travel stories I was used to reading.

Their accounts didn't focus so much on what they had done as on the people they had met, and on those people's most unforgettable stories. By turning their spotlight on others, the Gailles illuminated a wide and wondrous world that was new to me—and in so doing, they renewed my sense of just how rich and varied our planet is.

As I worked with Gina and Scott, I felt like I was journeying deeper and deeper into an enchanted landscape. I met characters I could vividly imagine but had never met, listened to stories that I had never heard and that blazed new mind-trails for me.

Now, rereading the completed collection, I realize that while the Gailles may not be professional travel writers, their stories embody three of the greatest lessons I have learned from a lifetime of travel writing.

The first is that after all the monuments, markets, and museums, our most memorable travel experiences almost always involve the people we meet.

The second is that everyone has a story, and often the people we least suspect have the most fascinating stories.

The third is that if we approach people with respect and appreciation, they will warmly welcome us into their lives, with respect and appreciation too.

A fourth corollary truth that this book abundantly proves is that if we ask the right questions, in the right spirit, the world will grace us with tales that we could not have imagined in our wildest dreams.

That's finally why I love this book. In the age of the selfie and the social mediafication of the planet, it is profoundly refreshing to be reminded that our world is infinitely full of surprises, if only we open ourselves to them, and that the ultimate reward of travel is connection—and the resulting richer appreciation of the human map of the world.

Don George has been called "a legendary travel writer and editor" by *National Geographic*. He is the author of *The Way of Wanderlust: The Best Travel Writing of Don George* and Lonely Planet's *How to Be a Travel Writer*. He has been Global Travel Editor at Lonely Planet and Travel Editor for Salon.com and the *San Francisco Examiner/ Chronicle*. He is currently Editor at Large for *National Geographic Traveler*. Don has edited twelve award-winning travel anthologies, including *The Kindness of Strangers, An Innocent Abroad,* and *Travelers' Tales Japan*.

*Lemon Shark*

# 1. Shark Repellent

*Bora Bora*

WHEN PEOPLE PICTURE visiting Bora Bora, they imagine themselves lounging on a long white sand beach flanked by green palm trees, looking onto a turquoise lagoon. They don't see themselves being charged by a predatory shark. But that's exactly what happened to the unfortunate traveler in this tale.

This idyllic South Pacific island is surrounded by a ring of reefs, which creates a tranquil lagoon filled with coral and millions of fish. Local tour operators offer a variety of excursions that bring visitors face-to-face with its marine life. One of the most popular is the shark-viewing tour. The best place on the island to see these majestic creatures is the narrow channel connecting the lagoon with the Pacific. Tides rush in and recede through the pass, creating an expressway for marine life. The tidal migrations of fish also attract large sharks, which congregate to partake in a smorgasbord. We decided to take one of these tours, and on our way to the channel, asked our Shark Guide, "What's the strangest thing you've ever seen here?"

## The Shark Guide's Story

"The most common sharks at the channel are sickle fin lemon sharks," explained our Shark Guide. "These are not the little reef sharks that snorkelers often take pictures of on the lagoon's coral reefs. Lemon sharks reach upward of twelve feet in length.

"I once had a group of Japanese tourists, one of whom looked very nervous. In broken English, he kept asking about safety. First, he wanted to know if there was a diving cage.

"'Because the sharks have thousands of fish to eat,' I explained, 'there's no need for them to prey on humans.'

"Next, he asked whether anyone had been attacked by a shark there.

"'Only once,' I answered. 'A lemon shark bit a diver's arm, but he was not seriously injured.'

"That did not appear to calm him. He started shaking his head and looking even more distraught.

"When we reached the pass, I briefed everyone on how to behave around the sharks.

"'Enter the water quietly. No splashing. Move slowly. Breathe calmly. Don't make noises under the water.'

"The questioning tourist was visibly scared. He was the last one in the water, and by that time, everyone else in the group had already swum twenty yards from the boat. They were following a shark that was hunting prey in the channel. When I turned to check on the straggler, I saw another big lemon shark rising from the depths below him.

"Before I could get back and calm him down, the scared tourist saw it too. He flailed wildly with his arms and legs, doing exactly what we had cautioned everyone not to do. It was like watching a car accident happen. His convulsions attracted the shark, and caused it to move right at him, with some speed.

"Just when it looked like he would become the second Bora Bora victim, the tourist turned his back to the shark, pulled off his swimming trunks, and evacuated his bowels—right in the approaching shark's face. When the cloud of waste hit the shark, it shook its head wildly and then swam off as fast as it could.

"A nearby school of colorful trigger fish then descended to eat the tourist's waste. My guest furiously tried to slap away the feeding frenzy as their hungry little mouths harmlessly pecked at his most tender regions.

"I've been told that the best thing to do if a shark comes in for an attack is to strike it on the nose or gills. Dive shops also sell cans of shark repellent, which can be sprayed in the direction of an approaching shark. But I learned something new that day. If all else fails, just pull down your pants and make your own repellent!"

A few minutes later, we were anchored above the same spot where the Japanese tourist had chased off his shark. The water was crystal clear and deep, perhaps fifty feet. Within minutes of our jumping in, six large lemon sharks rose slowly from the depths, circling us. They were ten or twelve feet long, but they looked even bigger in the water. Our hearts pounded as they swam by us within arm's reach—and we understood why that Japanese tourist had used the most primitive of defenses.

*Sahara Desert*

# 2. Cobra Bird

*Sahara Desert*

AMERICAN BUSINESSMEN LOOKING to make investments in other nations often visit the American Embassy there. Ambassadors know more about the local politics than anyone. In the privacy and security of the Embassy's compound, the ambassador can speak frankly about the risks facing investors. The ambassador also may be joined by other economic and security personnel, who may be even more willing to share. These young diplomats spend months isolated in remote capitals. They are eager for new company—or at least a couple of drinks at the hotel bar.

One young diplomat from Nouakchott, Mauritania, had a particularly interesting assignment. She was an expert on the nation's interior security—near the borderlands of Mauritania, Mali, and Algeria. She had recruited several nomads, trying to build a network to alert her about militant activities. In doing so, she had spent several weeks traversing the Sahara on their camel caravans.

## The Diplomat's Story

"The strangest thing I ever did out there was eat cobra bird," she said. "Certain birds of prey in the Sahara hunt poisonous snakes, particularly cobras. These birds are routinely envenomed by their prey, over time building up an immunity. One of my nomads was fond of cobra birds, describing an extraordinary high that comes from eating their flesh. This presumably was due to the presence of low levels of snake venom in the bird.

"I asked the nomad whether it was dangerous to eat the cobra bird. He assured me that it was perfectly safe in small quantities. Each person in the caravan only eats a bite or two, sharing the bird among many. No one had ever died from ingesting the bird.

"On the last night I was in the desert, one of the nomad foragers came back with just such a cobra bird. The mangled carcass was spit-roasted on the fire, and small pieces of its flesh were passed around.

"While I was reluctant to partake, curiosity got the better of me. This was my one shot to experience something truly unique and extraordinary. So, I took my greasy piece and slowly ate it. The meat was unremarkable in its taste.

"I sat there by the fire, looking up at the stars, and waiting for something to happen. The first strange sensation came from my fingertips. They felt tingly. The prickles gradually became more intense until it felt like there was something alive under my skin. This crawling sensation then spread across my hands and marched up my arms. The same feelings repeated themselves in my toes, gradually moving up my legs. It felt like an army of ants was marching through my veins. It was a creepy feeling, but not at all painful.

"The next thing I experienced was a growing euphoria. It was a superb feeling of contentedness, complete satisfaction. All thoughts and worries evaporated. Time seemed to slow down, and I was aware of my heart beating. I could feel the pulse, pulse, pulse, of blood in my arms and legs.

"I lay back on a pillow and stared up at the sparkling heavens. I saw a shooting star cross the sky, but it was in slow motion and the fireworks of its tail seemed to last an eternity. Awash in pleasure, I fell into a deep sleep.

"The next morning, I awoke feeling refreshed. Never before had I experienced such a peaceful, restorative sleep."

*Hippo Carcass*

# 3. Contagions

*Botswana*

THERE'S ONLY ONE PLACE in Africa where four nations' borders come together—the "Four Corners." There, in the middle of the Zambezi River, the borders of Zimbabwe, Zambia, Namibia, and Botswana all converge a little upriver from Victoria Falls. To its west lies Chobe National Park, a flooded water world that is home to the largest elephant herd in Africa, which is estimated to number more than one hundred twenty thousand. It's a crossroads for animals and people—and contagions.

## Scott's Story

I was with my guide in Chobe and we were watching a large elephant herd pass before us when I asked him my favorite question, "What's the strangest thing you have ever seen?"

"It's a tie," he replied. "But both were caused by contagions. One I can tell you about, and the second I can still show you."

"Let's start with the telling," I said.

"I was with some young, rich Englishmen on a safari, and all of them were very drunk. We were off the beaten path, driving along the Chobe River, when we came across a huge hippo, dead and decaying on the bank. Dead animals in Chobe were common. What was strange was the scavengers were missing. No crocodiles. No hyenas. No jackals. Not even vultures. Usually, there would be scores of them. That's when I knew that something wasn't right.

"We pulled up next to the carcass to take a closer look. As soon as we stopped, the Englishmen all bounded out of the Land Rover. I yelled for them to come back to the vehicle. They refused. Then the drunkest one climbed up on top of the bloated hippo, flexing his biceps, and posing for pictures. No sooner had the camera clicked than the skin of the animal gave way beneath him. In an instant, half the Englishman had disappeared into the hippo carcass. He sank all the way up to his belly button.

"'Help me,' he screamed. But his friends thought it was all hilarious. They pointed and laughed and snapped pictures as the Englishman struggled to climb out of the hippo, rolling onto the dusty ground. He was covered with black blood and rot and smelled even worse than he looked. I brought the Englishman a towel and told the others to stay away from him. Then I radioed for a ranger.

"When the Chobe ranger arrived, he walked around the hippo, carefully inspecting its mouth, nostrils, and anus.

"'Do you see the blood coming from the orifices?' asked the ranger.

"I nodded.

"Then he said the dreaded word, 'Anthrax.'

"Even the young Englishmen knew what that meant. The ranger took the Englishman away in the bed of his truck. They went straight to the nearest hospital for disinfectant and antibiotics. All of us were given protective doses, too, just in case."

The second half of my guide's story came later that evening, as we drove toward Victoria Falls. He started by showing me the Four Corners ferry crossing, where semi-trucks were lined up for miles waiting their turn. The villages around the crossing catered to the delayed drivers' every need. They sold beer and food, and well, other things, too.

My guide took me for a walk through the nearest village. Kids surrounded us and pulled at our shirtsleeves.

"Look around," said my guide. "What's wrong with this village?"

I took in the scene. Kids, and more kids. And some old people here and there.

"Where are their parents?" I asked.

"They are missing," explained my guide. "You see, the women here used to sell themselves to the truck drivers. The truck drivers gave them AIDS, and then they infected their husbands."

He walked me across the other side of the village to its cemetery. Rows and rows of fresh graves climbed the hillside.

"There are the parents," he said.

This was one of the AIDS villages, where almost everyone was wiped out. The year was 2005—when AIDS deaths peaked at more than two million annually.

"There are many ways to die in Africa," said my guide.

*Muscat, Oman*

# 4. Honey of Man

*Oman*

THE MIDDLE EAST'S ECONOMIES are driven by petroleum, and many of its residents make good livings working for oil companies. During the holy month of Ramadan, Muslims fast during the day, and little business is done. When night falls, though, the feasting begins. Steaming buffets serve culinary delights. After everyone is satiated, businessmen retire to private tents where they smoke *shisha*. Tall water pipes filled with fruit-flavored tobacco are passed from person to person. It was in one of these Ramadan tents that an oil trader started talking about the old days, when he and his family still traded pearls.

The setting for his story was the Indian Ocean port town of Muttrah, located in northern Oman. It has long been a hub of strategic trade between Arabia, Africa, India, and China. Muttrah's Al Dhalam Souq—literally translated as the "Market of Darkness"—is believed to be the oldest souk in Arabia. Some say its name originates from its many African traders. More likely, it came from the narrow, crowded stalls, which required lanterns to navigate even in the middle of the day. Black magic also persisted there well into the 20th century—and perhaps it still does.

## The Pearl Trader's Story

"When I was a boy, there was no oil," the Pearl Trader said. "All we had were pearls.

"I awoke one morning with a terrible fever. The doctor visited me, and told my parents that it would be my last day among the living. I remember my parents arguing fiercely about 'the old ways.' Arabia's position on the Indian Ocean meant that its people often hedged their bets—praying to Allah but partaking in traditional medicines and consulting with 'witch doctors' from Africa and South Asia.

"My father took me on his dhow, and we sailed from Fujairah along the coastline to the Omani harbor of Muttrah. I was too weak to walk, so my father carried me through the Market of Darkness. In one of its blackest alleys, there was a secret passageway that opened into a hidden shop.

"Inside, it was like nothing I had ever seen before. From the floor to the ceiling, its walls were lined with jars of honey in all shapes and sizes. Only each jar contained something else immersed inside the honey—organs and body parts. I soon would learn these were all human.

"My father sat me down on some pillows and produced a velvet bag from his pocket. The contents were carefully poured onto the shopkeeper's scale. It was a fortune of glistening pearls. The shopkeeper nodded, and two of his helpers came over and slowly pushed aside a heavy table that sat in the middle of the room. Then they each grabbed a shovel and started to dig into the dirt floor, excavating a wooden trapdoor.

"I watched them lift the trapdoor, revealing the hidden basement. The shopkeeper and his helpers went down its ladder, lighting several lanterns. The next thing I knew, my father was passing me through the hole, into the shopkeeper's sticky hands.

"The flickering light shown on two stone bathtubs filled with honey. Beneath the honey's surface, I could make out the corpses of a man and woman. There also were several circular honey jars along the walls, each containing what appeared to be a severed head. In the middle of it all was a stone table with straps on it.

"The shopkeeper carried me to the table and stripped away my clothes. Once I was naked, my hands and feet were tied to the corners with leather straps. I wanted to resist, but I was so sick that my arms and legs could not respond. I was expecting to be killed, imagining that my head would soon be looking down on the room from a jar like the others.

"I tried to yell for my father, but the shopkeeper grabbed my mouth, silencing me. Then he affixed a funnel to it, forcing the end down my throat. Looking up, I could still see my father, gazing through the trap door.

"Two helpers brought over one of the circular jars containing a severed head. Then they started to pour its honey into the funnel. 'Swallow as fast as you can,' ordered the shopkeeper, as a waterfall hit my throat.

"I drank of it, sometimes choking, until my belly swelled. The shopkeeper's hand was pushing on my stomach the whole time. Just when I thought I was going to explode, he shouted, 'Now,' and the helpers started pouring the rest of the honey over my torso.

"I must have fainted then. The next thing I remember was being back on the boat, sailing through the Arabian Sea. My fever was gone. I felt invigorated and strong again.

"For many years, I wondered whether it was all a feverish hallucination that I had mistaken for memory. My father never spoke of that day again—until he was on his deathbed. Praying to Allah, he asked to be forgiven for making his son partake in such a terrible sin.

"'*It was all real,*' I remember thinking.

"Then my father asked me to come closer. He had something else to confess. After the honey treatment, the shopkeeper kept me there for another two days, waiting to see whether I lived or died. The shopkeeper's bargain was this. If I lived, the shopkeeper would be paid the pearls. If I died, he would keep my body—and the pearls would be refunded. I had been sold on contingency, likely to be carved up into pieces, dropped into honey, and served up on the black market."

# 5. Beware of Road Surprises

*Emirate of Sharjah*

TRAFFIC ACCIDENTS CONSISTENTLY RANK among the top three killers of Americans who live or travel abroad. During a typical year, about one hundred fifty Americans die on foreign roadways. In the United Arab Emirates, there are large signs warning drivers in both Arabic and English to "Beware of Road Surprises." But what exactly is a road surprise?

## Scott's Story

The rolling red sand dunes of the Emirates are a playground for Middle Eastern tourists. They rent high-performance 4x4s and drive them into the endless sands to "dune bash," sliding down their slopes at high speed. But they are not the only ones occupying the desert. Camel farmers have lived there for millennia, raising their stock around its many palm-lined oases. Once upon a time, only camels could navigate the deep sands. Now, camel farmers must worry about drunken teenagers mowing them down.

*United Arab Emirates*

One of my coworker's college-aged sons was visiting the Emirates from the United States with his fraternity brothers. They took the family 4x4 and headed into the desert for some dune bashing. Unfortunately, no one warned them about the camel farmers. As the students drove the two-lane road into the desert, unbeknownst to them, a camel farmer was perched on the top of a dune. He was watching each of the oncoming vehicles with binoculars, trying to identify "soft targets." The young Americans were marked.

Farther up the road, large dunes came right down to the road's shoulder on both sides, creating a perfect spot to launch a road surprise. Hiding there was the co-conspirator, a camel farmer lying in wait with his old, decrepit camel. Camels are large beasts, measuring six feet tall and weighing in at more than one thousand pounds. They also have tall spindly legs, which can result in their bodies sliding across the hood and colliding with the windshield.

As the American's 4x4 approached the big dune, the camel farmer whipped the beast, causing it to lope out onto the road— right in front of the oncoming vehicle. There was nowhere for the boys to go to miss it. High dunes surrounded both sides of the road. They hit their brakes as hard as they could, but still struck the hapless animal. It was killed, and the 4x4 was totaled—but fortunately, the occupants escaped uninjured.

Immediately upon the occurrence of the accident, the camel farmer called the local police station. In the United States, a collision between a vehicle and an animal might give rise to an insurance claim or lawsuit. But in other nations, including the Emirate of Sharjah, it's a criminal matter. The driver of the vehicle is presumed guilty and promptly thrown into jail. Release only comes after he pays the farmer for the dead camel. These payments are referred to as "blood money."

The amount of blood money paid is a private negotiation, but clearly, the camel farmer is advantaged. The longer it takes for the parties to agree on the blood money, the lengthier is the driver's jail sentence. How much would you pay to get out of a hot, stinking Middle Eastern jail cell? Would you be willing to wait around for a few days while an insurance company tried to bargain the price down? How could an American frat boy prove what a camel was worth?

Such was the case in this incident. As soon as the student was arrested and thrown in jail, the farmer butchered the camel and sold its remains to a meat market. All evidence of the camel's age and condition was destroyed. Of course, the farmer could then claim that the camel was in the prime of its life.

In the case of my colleague, the farmer took the scam one step farther. This was not only a young, "breeding" camel, but also a "racing camel." Arabs not only race horses. They also race camels. The animals are fast, reaching speeds of 40 miles per hour. Racing camels, like race horses, are more valuable. The farmer initially demanded more than $100,000. My colleague negotiated this amount down, but it was still a substantial payment to secure the boy's release. Beware of road surprises.

# 6. Feeding Frenzy

## *Galápagos Islands*

WHEN WE THINK OF THE Galápagos Islands, giant tortoises and the comic antics of blue-footed boobies come to mind. Yet the real foundation of the islands' diverse ecosystem is the ocean. In its waters, three currents converge—from the south comes the cold Humboldt Current; from the north, the warm Panama Current; and from the west, the deep Cromwell Current. Together, they cycle nutrients to the ocean's surface. All of this results in giant schools of fish, which feed birds and other predators.

Each day, our Galápagos excursions were a mix of both worlds: land and sea. Half the day was spent walking among the birds, sea lions, tortoises, and iguanas. The rest was in the ocean. We had two guides with us, Jose and Maria. We noticed that Jose refused to get into the water. Hearing Maria chastise him for "still being afraid," we asked Jose what had happened.

*Bait Ball*

## The Ex-Snorkeler's Story

"We were snorkeling in the channel between Santa Cruz and Baltra, close to the airport when I saw boobies and other birds striking the water in the middle of the pass. I was with one of my guests, and I suggested we paddle over to watch the feeding birds.

"As we approached, we learned what was attracting the birds. It was a bait ball—a concentrated swarm of fish packed into a spherical formation. The fish do this as a defensive mechanism when under attack. There were thousands, maybe tens of thousands, of fish in the school.

"The ball was just below the surface, with a diameter approaching 20 meters. We were observing it from the side. The birds would hit the water at high speed, leaving trails of bubbles behind them as they rocketed in search of a catch. Then the school shifted in our direction, and we found ourselves right on top of the bait ball.

"On every side of us, birds were crashing into the water. It was crazy. I was floating on the surface with my face in the water, thoroughly enjoying the show. As I gazed down on the silver mass, a hole opened in its center. It was no longer a ball but a donut, and I could see straight into the deep blue below.

"Then I saw something else coming through the hole toward me. It was the head of an enormous shark, its jaws wide open, heading straight up—nearly vertical in its ascent.

"Everything slowed down then. It was as if time froze. I remembered a boy I had bullied in grade school. I thought about my mother. She had wanted me to come to dinner the night before, but I blew her off, opting instead to go drinking with friends in Puerto Ayora.

"The last thing I saw was the shark's jaws tearing through an unlucky tuna. Then its nose struck me squarely in the chest, stealing my breath. Everything went white at that point. I don't remember what happened next."

"But I do," said his colleague, Maria. "I was in a nearby dinghy, watching the birds feeding. I was unaware of any danger until I saw Jose lifted completely out of the water. His whole body was balanced across the snout of a giant tiger shark.

"I turned on the engine and sped to them. In accordance with protocol, I rescued the guest first. He had not even seen the shark.

"Jose was not far away, floating on the surface. He was still moving but appeared to be in shock. He did not even raise his head as the boat approached. I had to pull on his wetsuit cable to get his attention."

"Maria helped me into the boat," said Jose, "and I was shivering, shaking. I couldn't get warm."

"He hasn't been in the ocean since," said Maria.

Our guides told us this story just minutes before we were to snorkel under the cliffs of North Seymour Island. This was a drift snorkel. No swimming is required because a dinghy drops you off and the current carries the snorkelers under high cliffs for a few miles to the finish point, where the boat picks you up again. Maria went in the water with us, leaving Jose to run the dinghy.

We had been in the water about three-quarters of an hour when we crossed a boulder and found ourselves face to face with our own shark—a ten-foot-long oceanic white tip. This was not the passive reef shark usually encountered in the islands, but a more aggressive species—like the tiger shark, rarely encountered by *Galápagos* snorkelers. There were dozens of sea lions in the water around us, and the white tip appeared to be hunting them.

The shark was initially startled, and it dove beneath us. The guide immediately raised her hand, calling for Jose and the dinghy. We stayed close together, turning in the water to ensure that we continued to face the white tip. The shark initially looked like it would ignore us and swim off, but then it came back at us. It continued to circle until the dinghy neared. Only then did it finally spook and race off into the deep.

# 7. No Snake Dies Before Midnight

*Kangaroo Island*

OF THE WORLD'S TEN MOST venomous snakes, seven live in Australia, including the tiger snake. While its name comes from specimens with a striped appearance, it can just as easily be black or mottled. In the absence of anti-venom, its bite is fatal to humans about half the time. Nonetheless, it's a protected species, and a steep fine awaits anyone who intentionally injures one.

We were touring Kangaroo Island, a remote Australian island in the Southern Ocean with our guide, Andrew. When we asked him about the strangest thing he had ever seen there, his answer featured a tiger snake.

## Andrew's Story

"I was leading a dozen visitors from Shanghai on a bush hike. These were sophisticated urbanites. The women were decked out in designer resort wear and sandals. The men were similarly

*Scott's Tiger Snake*

attired. They were wearing swim trunks, polo shirts, and flip flops. It looked like a fashion show—not a trek through the wild Australian bush.

"We were about a mile into the hike when I heard a chorus of laughter erupt behind me. I looked back to see that my group was engaged in a photography frenzy with each of them taking turns posing with one of the men.

"As I approached, I could see that the man had his foot on something, and it was moving. That something was a snake.

"'Crikey!' I yelled and ran back to them.

"My guest had one of his flip flops firmly planted on the tail of a tiger snake. The tiger snake was writhing and twisting, trying its best to get away—while the Chinese were live-streaming the spectacle.

"Only one woman in the group was fluent in English. I walked up to her and whispered calmly in her ear, 'Do exactly what I say. This is a matter of life and death. That's a deadly snake. I need you to tell the one with his foot on the snake to keep absolutely still, and the others, to slowly back away.'

"As she translated what I had said, the laughter stopped instantly. Everyone looked like death. Meanwhile, the tiger snake was still trying to crawl away. Fortunately, it had not yet decided to turn around and bite its captor.

"I spoke again to the translator, 'Now tell him to very slowly lift off his foot and release the snake.'

"She translated to him, and he spoke back to her in quavering Chinese, but he did not lift up his foot.

"'He is afraid the snake will turn around and bite him,' she replied. Literally, he had a tiger by the tail.

"'Tell him that it can turn around and bite him right now, and that it is going to do so if he does not immediately release it.'

"She translated for me, and the flip flop ever so slowly lifted itself from the tiger snake's tail. The snake accelerated off, across the trail, and into the bush as fast as it could go.

"My guest was shaking so that he had to sit down in the middle of the trail to collect himself. The others gathered around him, and now they were laughing again.

"I pulled the woman aside and asked her why he had done that. She replied, 'He wanted a picture with the snake for his Instagram and was afraid it was going to get away.'"

## Gina's Story

The next day we were driving to the airport with Andrew when we heard a thump under the right tire.

"Snake," he shouted, bringing the Land Rover to a halt.

We got out and walked back down the road. Sure enough, there was a large tiger snake on its back, lying completely motionless. I watched Scott pick up a stick and walk over to the snake. He poked the snake. It didn't move.

"That's not a good idea," I said.

"Keep your distance," Andrew cautioned.

"It's dead," said Scott, who then used the branch to flip the snake over for a better look.

No sooner had Scott righted the snake than it came back to life and started slithering again.

Scott jumped back, putting some much-needed space between him and the tiger snake.

"Must have just been stunned," Scott said.

"Tiger snakes are tough," Andrew said. "The aborigines have a proverb about apparently dead snakes still being dangerous. They say that 'no snake dies before midnight.' The aborigines leave a snake where it has fallen overnight—just to make sure it really is dead."

# 8. The Emperor Has No Underwear

*United Arab Emirates*

HANS CHRISTIAN ANDERSEN'S TALE *The Emperor's New Clothes* has delighted children for almost two centuries. The tale's Emperor is tricked into believing that he has been sold the finest suit in the world—made of fabric invisible to those who are unworthy. All of the Emperor's ministers say nothing and allow him to parade around in his new outfit. Then a child blurts out, "But he isn't wearing anything at all!"

Business leaders, too, can succumb to imperial ambitions. This is doubly true in the Middle East, where CEOs cavort with real kings and sultans. CEOs make millions of dollars a year. Middle Eastern sheikhs make millions of dollars a day. Still, the CEOs try to keep up, and that leads to strange behavior. The young vice president of an oil company often traveled as part of his CEO's entourage. He was there when his emperor ran out of underwear.

*Falcon Hunting*

## The Vice President's Story

"I was sitting at the back of a triangular conference room. My CEO was holding court at the apex of the room, where the panes of glass met to form a perfect point. Behind him was the endless blue of the Persian Gulf, broken only by dozens of oil tankers chugging to and from the Strait of Hormuz. To his right was the CEO of another company. Both men had just arrived from America in their own private planes.

"'I'm still waiting on my wife,' complained the second CEO.

"'She didn't fly in with you?' asked the first.

"'No. Since the Tyco scandal, she's been flying commercial, mostly using air miles.'

"After their meeting adjourned, my CEO pulled me aside and asked, 'What are airline miles?' I explained to him how airlines have loyalty programs pursuant to which members receive points based on how far they fly each year. These 'air miles' can then be redeemed for free tickets. 'Fascinating system,' he said. 'I haven't flown commercially since the 1970s. There were no air miles back then.'

"Just as suburban dads might compare the automatic sliding doors on their minivans, so do CEOs brag about their planes. These babies are not just little Lear jets, but rather Boeing Business Jets, or BBJs—customized 737s, 767s, or 777s. They are outfitted with queen size beds, hot showers, and extra fuel tanks to extend their range to the farthest corners of the world.

"Yet I was not allowed on my CEO's BBJ. Even when we traveled together, he would board his BBJ, and I would be relegated to one of the company's smaller Gulfstream jets. The two planes would take off together, one after another, and then fly the same route. It was all such a waste.

"That night, the Sheikh hosted everyone for dinner at his palace. At the event's conclusion, he invited the CEOs to join him on a falcoln hunting trip in Pakistan. I thought nothing of it until my boss's secretary knocked on my hotel room door.

"'We have a problem,' she said. 'The boss does not have enough underwear for the hunting trip.'

"'So, our Emperor has no underwear. Why's that a problem?' I asked, handing her a sheet showing prices for the hotel's one-hour laundry service.

"'That won't do,' she said. 'He's worried about germs. The boss would never allow his underwear to be cleaned by a public facility.'

"'Are we working for Howard Hughes?' I asked. 'Why don't you go down to the two hundred-store mall and buy some new underwear?'

"'I already tried that. No one has his brand. Not here. Not even in Dubai.'

"'And what brand might that be?' I asked.

"'Hermes.'

"'Like my ties?' I asked. 'I didn't even know they made underwear.'

"'It's the only brand he'll wear. Hermes boxer shorts.'

"'I don't suppose you could persuade him to cycle through the ones he brought.'

"'Not going to happen,' she replied. 'The closest location that carries his underwear is the Hermes store in Paris.'

"'Perfect. Just have them FedExed down.'

"'There's not time. The only way is to fly there ourselves tonight, buy them when the store opens, and then fly right back.'

"'Have fun with that,' I said. 'That's three thousand miles each direction—twelve hours flying round trip.'

"'It's you who's going to Paris to get the underwear,' she said. 'He sent me to tell you that the pilots are fueling the BBJ now.'

"Instead of attending the rest of the meetings in Abu Dhabi, my Wharton MBA was put to its highest and best use of making an underwear run. It was the only time I ever set foot on my boss's BBJ, but I made the most of it. I napped on his plush bed, took a shower in his flying bathroom, watched movies on the big screen TV, ate his caviar, and drank his 19th-century cognac. My trip was a success, and the Imperial CEO was able to continue on his hunting trip with a suitcase full of brand-new Hermes boxer shorts."

*Lagos, Nigeria*

# 9. Road Warrior

*Nigeria*

With more than twenty million people, Lagos, the business capital of Nigeria, is the largest city in Africa. It's also a city of extremes. It hosts four billionaires and thousands of million-aires—*ajebotas* or "butter eaters." At the opposite end are several million unemployed—the *ajepakos* or "twig eaters." Desperation in proximity to such extreme wealth has pitted the twig eaters against the butter eaters.

The personal security of the butter eaters is largely a private affair. The U.S. Department of State explains that a "serious lack of resources (communications equipment, vehicles, skilled lead-ership, training) continues to undermine the effectiveness of the Nigeria Police Force (NPF).... Criminal groups do not fear arrest or prosecution for their crimes. Local police and neighborhood associations, including vigilante groups, generally do not deter or disrupt crimes and seldom apprehend or detain suspects." *The*

*Economist* magazine describes how "commuters in even the poshest parts of town are sometimes caught in shoot-outs between robbers and policemen," leading to Lagos being ranked among the five least livable cities in the world—alongside war-torn Damascus and Tripoli.

Scott asked a food executive who frequently travels to Lagos on business what was the strangest thing he had ever seen there. His story only serves to reinforce Lagos's dangerous reputation.

## The Road Warrior's Story

"I regularly travel to Lagos to oversee our Nigeria operations," said the Road Warrior. "We employ many thousands of Nigerians at our plants, and Africa is one of my company's principal growth markets.

"The routine is always the same. I arrive in the evening, and it's dark by the time I get through customs. I'm met there by a driver and an armed security guard. The security guard rides in the front seat while I work on my laptop in the back. I had made the trip dozens of times without incident. This time it would be different.

"We hadn't been driving for long when I heard the *rat-a-tat-tat* of machine gun fire alongside my car. I looked out the window, and there riding beside me was a pickup truck filled with masked men. The two in its bed were armed with AK-47s. They were firing their weapons into the air—the muzzle flashes so close and bright as to leave me seeing spots.

"My driver slammed on the brakes and screeched to a stop on the side of the road, causing the pickup to pass us by. Then I saw smoke from its tires, as the gang hit the brakes hard, too. Without saying a word to me, my driver and guard opened their doors and sprinted off into the darkness in opposite directions. They had left me behind. I was frozen. The truck of gangsters was backing up fast. It was too late for me to run.

"I stepped out of the car with my hands up, looking down. In Nigeria, both robbers and murderers faced the prospect of the death penalty. This created a perverse incentive for thieves to kill those who could identify them.

"Two men with guns pushed me onto the roadside, while others climbed into my car and sped away.

"'Phone, wallet, watch, and shoes!' the leader shouted at me.

"I silently complied, passing them the first three, and then slipping my loafers off and handing those over as well."

"'Take off your clothes!' was the next order.

"I took off everything but my boxer shorts and socks and handed them over.

"'The shorts and socks, too!'

"'Really, man?' I asked, glancing up at the man's face for the first time. He was wearing a ski mask. 'Please, no.'

"The sweating masked man leveled the AK-47 at my face. I took off my underwear and socks and was now completely naked.

"'The ring, too!' he shouted, apparently just noticing my simple wedding band.

"I reached down to pull it off, but my fingers were swollen from the flight, and I couldn't get it over my knuckle.

"'It won't come off.'

"The second assailant threw his AK-47 over his shoulder and grabbed my finger. He yanked so hard on the ring, I thought he would pull my finger off. Yet it still didn't budge.

"'Cut it off!' shouted the leader.

"His second sprinted over to the pickup truck. After fumbling in the back, he came back with a pair of rose clippers.

"I mustered up all the spit my adrenalin-dried mouth had to offer and twisted like hell, managing to painfully pop the ring free. As soon as I handed it over, they drove away.

"The good news was that they hadn't hurt me. The bad news was that I was alone and naked on the side of the road. There was a steady stream of vehicles coming from the airport. I tried to get one to help me. Not one stopped, though. So, I started walking back to the airport. It was a few miles of humiliation, but after a while I forgot about being naked. My biggest concern was trying to dodge broken glass and other trash alongside the road. When I finally reached the airport guards, they did not appear the least bit surprised.

"As soon as they saw me, one of them yelled, 'It's another naked white guy.'"

# 10. Agent Ghost

*Somewhere in Africa*

RETIRED CIA AND SECRET INTELLIGENCE SERVICE agents often find second careers in the private sector, working for companies rather than governments. Their help is particularly valuable in nations where they previously operated. These former agents can tap into their old networks for two business purposes—securing meetings and obtaining intelligence about government actions.

Agent Ghost was working for a private intelligence firm when Scott met him, but before that, he had spent many decades serving Great Britain in Africa's hot spots. Britain in particular has a controversial history in Africa. Among other covert actions, its agents have been accused of assassinating Patrice Lumumba, then Prime Minister of the Democratic Republic of Congo—to prevent the nation's uranium mines from falling into the hands of communists. Agent Ghost was of Scottish lineage and looked a lot like Sean Connery, with one glaring exception. He

*Destroyed Tank in Central Africa*

had matching scars on each of his cheeks. Most people who met Agent Ghost assumed they were ritual scars, given as a badge of honor, perhaps by an African chief. The truth was something entirely different.

## Agent Ghost's Story

"A civil war was raging across central Africa," Agent Ghost explained. "It was the clash of civilizations—Soviet communism versus western capitalism. We were helping the good guys when one of my local operatives betrayed me to the communists. Rebels kicked in my door in the middle of the night.

"I got off a couple of shots, but there were too many of them. That's where the movies get it wrong. Sheer numbers usually prevail. In a matter of seconds, I was hit over the head and knocked unconscious. I woke up to find myself blindfolded in the trunk of a car, my hands tied behind my back.

"When the vehicle finally stopped, my assailants opened the trunk and pulled me out. I couldn't see a thing, but the stench was awful. As they led me up a hill, I could feel and hear the crunching of garbage. I remember thinking: This is not good. This is how it's going to end.

"I wasn't going to make it any easier so I went limp. It would buy me a few more minutes of life. They cursed me, but it didn't change the outcome. They dragged me through the foulest of refuse. We went up and then down the trash hill before they stopped and pulled me to my knees.

"'Take off his blindfold,' said the voice of my former operative.

"When they did, I found myself in a valley of garbage. The Judas was in front of me, smiling slyly, and looking quite smug.

"'So much for the big man,' he said.

"Whether it was my concussion or the rotten smell, I vomited, spraying Judas's trousers in front of me.

"'Get it over with,' he shouted, and then he turned and walked away.

"One of his men pulled my blindfold back over my eyes. The nausea wave came again, and just as I heaved, something hit me in the side of my face. I don't even remember hearing the gun go off. There was just a jerk to my head followed by a searing pain. The men released me, and I fell sideways into the garbage. My mouth tasted of blood and gunpowder. In all my years of service, that was the first time I had ever been shot. Even though I knew it was coming, the feeling of dread was overwhelming. I was confused, but I knew I didn't want them to shoot me again. So, I lay very still, trying to remember a woman I had loved. The thought of her calmed me enough.

"I tried to listen for my executioner walking away or the car driving away. But one of my ears was pressed against filth and the other was rendered deaf by the gunshot. So, I just stayed still, replaying the memories of my woman. She would be my last thought when I died. Only death did not come, and I actually started feeling a little better.

"The first thing I moved was my mouth, and the pain made me see stars. I'd been shot in the mouth. I moved my tongue around, finding the broken shards of molars, the entry hole, and the gash in my cheek where the bullet and several shattered teeth had exited. Then I rubbed my head against the trash until my blindfold slid off.

"I rolled over onto my knees and spit out a mouthful of blood, along with pieces of teeth. My jaw hurt, but I could move it up and down. Once I was righted, I could hear again, too, albeit only with one ear. There was nocturnal foraging not far away.

Thinking it might be hyenas or worse, I found a piece of broken bottle and cut through the rope holding my hands. Reaching up to my face, I felt the two holes, one in each cheek.

"I used the last hour of darkness to walk back to my apartment, where I had a sewing kit. I cleaned and sutured my wounds. Then it was time to go hunting.

"Judas pissed his pants when he saw me, uttering the word 'ghost.' The coward gave up his accomplices before he met the fate he had intended for me.

"I spent the rest of the morning tracking down the others, letting each see me for a second or two before I killed them. Just long enough for them to mutter, or in one case, only mouth, 'ghost.'

"I went on to help our man win his civil war, and a few years later, Reagan and Thatcher won their Cold War, banishing communism to the garbage dump of history."

*Breakfast on Safari*

# 11. Here, Little Birdie

*Kenya*

MORNING GAME DRIVES IN AFRICA depart in the wee hours of the morning. It's not unusual to be roused from tents at 5 a.m., handed a cup of coffee, and then sent bouncing along in an open Land Rover. After all, the animals are most active at dawn and dusk. By 9 a.m. or so, wildlife has retreated to dense foliage, preparing to escape the coming heat. That's the perfect time for a proper breakfast. While guests sip on champagne and orange juice, the lodge's cook builds a campfire and fries bacon and eggs. Scott asked the cook what was the strangest thing a visitor had ever done on safari.

## The Cook's Story

"We were with a group of serious bird-watchers. They didn't want to see lions. All they wanted to do was count birds. While we were eating breakfast, a rare hawk was swooping over us, trying to steal some of our food. It would land and then fly away, coming back again and again. I tried to scare it off, but one of the guests asked me to let it come in closer.

"On its next landing, it walked right up to us. One member of the group tossed it a piece of bacon, which the hawk quickly devoured before taking wing.

"'Watch this,' said the man, who put a piece of bacon on top of his bald head.

"'Here, little birdie,' the man called out, trying to lure the hawk closer.

"The hawk circled us, eyeing the bacon prize.

"Then it came in real slow—and hovered above the man's shoulder.

"'It's going to land on me,' he boasted, as the others snapped pictures.

"His words scared the bird, and it flew off.

"We were all looking around for it, trying to figure out where it had gone.

"'Here it comes again,' said one of the others.

"'Where?' asked the man. 'I don't see it.'

"Then I saw it coming. The hawk was swooping in from behind the man. But instead of landing, the hawk accelerated, using its talons to pluck the bacon from the man's head. In that instant, I ducked—half expecting the bird was going to strike me next.

"When I glanced back, the bird watcher was looking down, and across his bald scalp were two long gashes from the hawk's talons. As he lifted his head, streams of blood flowed down his face.

"We grabbed the first aid kit and applied pressure. But it was worse than a cut. The hawk had ripped away some of his flesh—all the way to the bone. His wounds were so bad that he had to be evacuated to London for surgery."

# 12. The Human Pet

*Qatar*

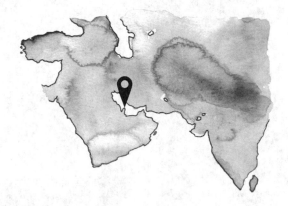

QATAR IS THE WORLD'S RICHEST NATION—per capita. Its quarter million citizens are ruled by the House of Thani, the current Emir being the eighth in a two hundred-year royal lineage. The Thanis preside over twenty-five billion barrels of oil and gas. Westerners seeking to raise capital for their businesses routinely travel to Qatar's capital, Doha, in search of Thani patronage. One such businessman's stay in Qatar lasted much longer than he had expected. A prince enjoyed the American so much that he invited him to live at his palace.

## The Pet's Story

"Each morning, the Prince would join me for breakfast beside his Olympic-sized swimming pool. Servants brought me whatever I ordered. Then the Prince would take hold of my arm and start his day. Most mornings we began with online shopping.

*The Rulers of Qatar*

We'd participate in auctions of art and antiques at Sotheby's and Christie's. He had an insatiable appetite for buying. Tens of millions of dollars were spent without thinking twice.

"Around midday, the delivery trucks started to arrive, depositing the bounty of the Prince's purchases along his circular driveway. We sat in his Rolls Royce convertible, watching as servants used crowbars to pry crate after crate open. Each item was shown to the Prince before being taken away.

"The Prince bought so much, so fast, that he actually forgot what he had ordered. It was like watching a kid at Christmas, opening presents, one after another. His attention span also resembled that of a child. He looked at each treasure for only a minute before moving on to the next one.

"Lunch in the Prince's grand dining room invariably followed the openings. Every wall was covered with inlaid marble. Artisans from India, who were taught in the arts of the Taj Mahal, had been imported to create this masterpiece anew.

"After lunch, the Prince wandered around the palace. I followed at his side. These afternoons served no purpose other than the passing of time. The Prince went from room to room, rummaging through his collections of art and artifacts. Each room had a theme—for example, 19th-century Impressionist paintings—but the contents seemed haphazard, even chaotic. Instead of being hung, paintings leaned against the walls in giant stacks, dozens of canvases deep. To view them, servants would shuffle the frames, bringing each to the Prince until he sent it back. There were many Monets and Renoirs, but the Prince didn't even seem to recognize, much less appreciate, the artists. They were just pretty things that he owned.

"The price of all things seemed inconsequential to the Prince. This was because he had an endless fountain of money that replenished itself as he spent. Whether a thing cost $100 or $100 million, it made no difference to his wealth. He was on a perpetual shopping spree. The absence of relative sacrifice—that the rest of us experience—had left the Prince unable to appreciate the value of anything.

"When the Prince got tired of looking at his possessions, he would take me for a swim in his chilled pool. On really hot days, the servants would bring large blocks of ice and drop them one after another into its waters to further cool them. I tried to use the pool as a place to discuss my business investment with the Prince, but he always found a way to delay and defer any commitment.

"Each day led into another, until I had been at the palace for two months straight. Repetition does make time fly. We had returned again to the room of Impressionist paintings. The giddy Prince had his servants shuffling them, just as he had done before. It was then that I realized I was the Prince's Pet—just like a dog, following his owner around.

"The next day, my monotony was broken when an order of antique shotguns arrived. I'm an avid bird hunter so I was particularly enjoying them. While I was examining my favorite over-under, the Prince mentioned that his estate was home to flocks of doves. He suggested that we go bird hunting together and put the purchase to use.

"That evening we were dropped off at two separate locations, out of sight from each other. Servants clambered through nearby bushes, flushing the doves and causing them to fly over. I was having a great time, blasting away. In addition to shooting many doves, I also bagged several larger pigeons. The only odd thing about the pigeons was that they were all tagged with gold bracelets containing Arabic writing around their legs.

"When we arrived back in the palace's courtyard, we found a great commotion. The courtyard was packed with vehicles, and dozens of men were looking skyward with binoculars. The Prince went over to talk to an older gentleman, who was holding his head with both hands and looking distraught. Upon seeing me arrive, the Prince hurried me away from the scene.

"'What's wrong?' I asked.

"The Prince described how the Emir's prized racing pigeons had gone missing. They were participating in a competition and disappeared as they were flying across the property.

"I got a sinking feeling in my stomach.

"'Dump out your birds,' demanded the Prince. I sheepishly did so, spilling a pile of carcasses onto the grass. The evidence was indisputable. The Prince picked out ten pigeons, each with a gleaming gold band, and numbered (in Arabic) one to ten.

"'How did you manage to kill them all?' exclaimed the Prince.

"I shrugged. 'I'm a good shot.'

"Later that night, I was taken to the airport and put on the next flight to London—in economy class."

*Monitor Lizard*

# 13. That's Not a Rubber Ducky

*Equatorial Guinea*

EQUATORIAL GUINEA IS A SMALL NATION on the West African coast, with its territory divided between the African mainland and a volcanic island in the Atlantic Ocean. Prior to the discovery of oil, conditions were so poor that the country could barely afford to run its electric plants. Blackouts were common, and the President would order the electricity plants shut down whenever he traveled abroad. The President once quipped, "This is my house, and I can turn off the lights if I want." That all changed in 1995, with the discovery of large oil and gas fields. Over the next fifteen years, the nation's gross domestic product per person increased more than seventy-fold.

## The Partner's Story

After oil was discovered, high-priced lawyers descended on EG to negotiate petroleum concessions. They encountered one of the hardships of petro-travel—the absence of comfortable hotels. Everyone shared the same vermin-infested dormitories. These facilities also lacked private bathrooms, and community showers were the norm.

"My EG dorm had one shower room," the Partner explained. "There were several showerheads on the wall so that multiple guests could bathe simultaneously—cold water only. It was like being in high school gym class again. The room had no artificial lights, but it did have a large window that opened onto the jungle behind the dorm. A couple of vines had grown through the slats of the rotting hurricane shutters. Worst of all was its sunken floor. The central drain barely functioned, leaving behind a fetid pond.

"On the morning in question," the Partner said, "I walked down the hall at dawn hoping for some privacy. I stepped into scummy, ankle-deep water. Although I usually wore glasses, I had left them behind on my bunk. Not seeing clearly made the standing water seem cleaner than it was.

"Just a few seconds after I turned on the shower, the shutter swung wide open. There was something in the window, climbing over the ledge. It was large, too. The outline of a long tail was the last thing I saw before it plopped into the standing water, joining me. I pivoted toward the doorway, but the creature had beaten me there. It was now perched on the steps, blocking my escape.

"I called for help, meekly at first. Then I called for help louder, finally getting the attention of another lodger. He opened the door, sending more light onto the shower steps and the creature. It was an enormous monitor lizard, as long as me. The guest shouted an obscenity in French and fled down the hall. I moved toward the lizard, but I must have gotten too close because it started hissing at me.

"The cavalry was coming to my rescue, though. Just behind the lizard were two approaching Africans, one with a wooden club. They motioned for me to back up, which I did slowly. Then the one with the club sprang forward, smashing the creature atop its head. While the first blow was probably sufficient, he didn't let up, smacking the lizard again and again, splattering blood across my naked body. When the carnage ceased, the second man poked the lizard a couple of times with a broom to ensure it was dead. Then they rolled it over, lashed its front and hind legs to the broom's stick, and hauled it off.

"That night, the dormitory's chef roasted the monitor lizard and served it up as the 'catch of the day.' It tasted just like chicken."

*Great White Shark Breaching*

# 14. Great White Shark Buffet

*Southern Ocean*

GANSBAAI IS LOCATED ON THE southern coast of South Africa, looking towards Antarctica. About five miles offshore lie two small islands, Geyser Rock and Dyer Island, which are inhabited by more than sixty thousand fur seals and a colony of penguins. The channel between these islands is known as Shark Alley. An estimated one thousand great white sharks converge on the islands to feed on the seals and penguins. This feeding frenzy often results in the giant sharks using an attack technique in which they swim upward from below at such speed that they breach the surface, completely leaving the water. After the Discovery Channel featured these sharks as "Air Jaws," local boat owners soon started offering tours of Shark Alley.

## Scott's Story

I was in Cape Town meeting with the South African Petroleum Agency when I visited Gansbaai and joined one of its shark diving tours. I was whisked out to sea on a rubber skiff, bouncing over large swells to reach a dive boat moored in Shark Alley. As my skiff approached, I saw a giant fin cutting through the clear water alongside me. The great white dove and passed underneath us—all fifteen feet of it.

"The swells are too large for us to tie-off," said the skiff driver, shaking his head.

"Do we have to go back?" I asked.

"No, we'll just hand you over," he said.

"You'll do what?" I asked.

Before I even realized what was about to happen, the skiff driver gunned the boat and came alongside the mother ship. A burly crew member from the dive ship reached both of his hands in my direction as we approached.

"Grab his hands!" shouted the skiff driver.

I reached up, and as our hands locked, I was lifted off the skiff and against the railing of the big boat. For a couple of seconds, my legs freely dangled above the ocean as the skiff fell away. Then the crewman hoisted me over the rails and safely onto the boat.

"Have you ever lost anyone with that maneuver?" I asked him when I caught my breath.

He laughed. "No, we do it all the time. It's safer than it seems."

"Here, put these on," he said, handing me a mask, snorkel, and heavy wetsuit. "The water temperature is 16 degrees C, or about 59 degrees F."

After putting my gear on, I was helped down a ladder at the stern of the boat into a floating shark cage.

"Keep your hands and feet inside the cage at all times!" he shouted. "Do not grab onto the railing."

When I splashed into the Southern Ocean, the cold was such a shock that it took my breath away. It felt like ice water!

"Ready, set, go!" shouted the crewman, as he used a long pole to push the cage away from the boat. It floated off about twenty yards before the mooring rope held tight.

I was treading water on the surface, inside the cage, as swells bobbed me up and down. My heart was pounding from the cold and sea conditions. Then it pounded even harder when a large fin broke the surface only ten yards away. Even though I was safely in a cage, the sight of the fin affected me.

"Head in the water!" yelled the crewman from the mother ship. "Hold your hands against your chest!"

I put my mask down and looked into the clear green water. Before me was the back end of the shark swimming off into the distance. Then there was a splash right next to me. It was a rope holding the head of a big fish thrown from the dive boat.

The shark that had been swimming away then turned around and came back my way. It was heading straight for the bleeding fish head. After that, everything happened in slow motion. Its jaws opened, giant teeth bared, and then it bit down on the fish head, shaking and chewing away.

I was so enthralled by the action that I didn't even consider what would happen next. The great white slammed into the cage at speed—just inches in front of me. So much for holding my hands against my chest. There was a bar above me, and I instinctively surfaced and grabbed it, trying to steady myself. I held on to the crossbar as the creature's immense weight drove the cage, and me, through the ocean. When the cage stopped moving, I put my face back underwater. The great white was still there, slowly passing alongside me. I reached out through the bars and touched its side, letting my fingers drag along its skin as it swam away.

This feeding routine continued for twenty minutes. Sharks were lured to the cage by chum, but only twice was the cage struck. The second time I kept my head in the water, watching the great white's chomping jaws press the tuna against the bars. Its teeth were so close, only a foot or two away from me. I could even hear them scraping against the cage.

After that, I was reeled back to the boat and pulled from the ocean. When I climbed out, I started shivering uncontrollably.

"Your lips are blue," said the captain, passing me a blanket and taking me into his cockpit to warm me up.

"Just watch the horizon between here and the island," he explained. "You'll see the sharks surface when they attack a seal or penguin."

Since the breaching sharks were attacking vertically, from underneath, there was never any indication of where they would emerge. The water would just randomly explode upwards, and there would be a great white shark flying out of the water. A couple of times, I could even see the prey dangling from its jaws.

As I watched in the cockpit, the crewman who had pulled me aboard sat down and opened a beer. It was time for my favorite question.

"What's the strangest thing you've ever seen out here?" I asked.

The crewman rubbed his chin and then started. "We try to keep the bait close to the cage for two reasons. You get to see the action, and it makes the sharks attack sideways. If the fish is thrown too short, we have to pull it back and throw it again— otherwise, there's the risk the shark will attack from below, and we never know where its one thousand kilograms will land.

"There were four divers in the cage when we had a bum throw. The fish ended up well off to the side. The thrower immediately realized his error and started to pull it back. He didn't make it far before a four-meter shark hit the bait from below. It happened so fast there was nothing we could do. The beast flew into the air and then landed squarely atop the cage. If a shark can feel pain, this one certainly did. He stopped moving altogether, and just hung limp—half in and half out of the water, suspended across the cage. For a moment, I thought the collision had killed it.

"The divers immediately surfaced around the shark. One of the ladies started screaming. Her ear-piercing shrieks reawakened the shark, and it did a sort of shake and flop, before rolling back into the ocean. In the process, the great white knocked off half of the cage's floats, causing it to partially sink beneath the surface.

"The divers were calling for us to reel them in. They held on to the side that was partially floating, but they were still exposed on the other side. A shark with the right angle of attack could easily have come in and taken one of our guests. To keep the sharks away, we chummed the water on the far side of the dive boat, successfully luring them away long enough for us to complete the rescue."

A few years after my shark diving experience, I read about a tragic accident at Shark Alley. A moored dive boat was hit by a rogue wave coming out of the Southern Ocean. The wave capsized the vessel, spilling everyone into the shark-infested waters. Two Americans and one Norwegian lost their lives in the accident.

*Taquile Island, Peru*

# 15. UFOs

*South America and Caribbean Sea*

NOT LONG AGO, THE UNITED STATES government declas-
sified decades of military research into unidentified flying
objects—"UFOs." The report concluded that there was no evidence to indicate that any of the incidents were the result of
extraterrestrial visitors. Half of humanity now carries around
smartphones equipped with video cameras. If extraterrestrials
were visiting our planet, someone, somewhere, would have them
on video. Nevertheless, our question, "What's the strangest thing
you've ever seen?" has resulted in a few memorable UFO stories.

## The Guide's Story

"I was a teenager. It was not long after dark, and we were playing
soccer in a field on the shore of Lake Titicaca. Over the lake
we saw a bright light, as large as the full moon. It moved slowly

across the sky, rapidly changing colors—all the colors of the rainbow. Then it flashed a blinding white and went straight up, disappearing into space.

"About a decade later, I was working for an old man on Taquile Island in the middle of the lake. He had lived on Lake Titicaca all his life. It was a clear and still night, and we were sitting on a hill, admiring the heavens. I told him my story of the light and asked whether he had ever seen anything like it. The old man smiled knowingly. He had.

"'When I was a child,' he said, 'my brother fell ill. A doctor came to see him and told us he would not make it. There was nothing more that could be done for him.

"'In the middle of the night, a strange noise woke me up. *Whoosh, whoosh, whoosh.* I sat up in bed and looked out the window. *Whoosh, whoosh, whoosh.* The hillside was illuminated with a brilliant white light—just like you had described. Then it was gone. I tossed and turned for a while but eventually fell back to sleep.

"'The next morning, I was awakened in bed by my brother. He was shaking me. He looked completely healthy. He excitedly told me how two funny-looking doctors with big heads came to visit him during the night. He claimed that they had shined lights on him, curing him. My parents dismissed it as a feverish dream. But I had heard and seen something inexplicable that night, too.'"

## The Captain's Story

"Charter boat captains are not allowed to have any alcohol in their body while at the helm. Safety's a high priority in the Virgin Islands, and we're routinely given sobriety checks after pulling into port. Drinking means risking the loss of my license—my livelihood. It's just not worth it. What I want you to know is that my senses were unimpaired when I saw it.

"On the day in question, I was at the helm of a chartered sailboat, passing over one of the deepest spots in the world's oceans—the Puerto Rico Trench. I was scanning the horizon in search of whales when something caught my eye. About fifty yards behind the boat I saw a car-sized sphere hovering just above the cobalt waves. It had an iridescent sheen, rather like a soap bubble.

"At first, I thought it was a natural phenomenon. Whales sometimes emit giant bubbles as they dive. Maybe this was an oily whale burp? Only it wasn't dissipating. The Bubble was following my boat—at the exact same speed. It seemed reflective, mirroring the waves and sky around it. I changed course, and so did the Bubble. It continued to follow. As it moved in front of distant clouds, I realized the Bubble was transparent. I was looking right through the thing.

"I called my passengers over. They saw it, too. I wasn't hallucinating. When one of them tried to snap a photo, the Bubble reacted immediately. It turned and accelerated away, flying across the water and disappearing over the horizon.

"I spent the next few days on the Internet, searching for answers. I read a lot about the Puerto Rico Trench. It's the deepest point in the Atlantic Ocean at more than twenty-eight thousand feet. American submarines use the depths for training, and it's the fictional location in Tom Clancy's novel for the scuttling of the Soviet submarine, *Red October*.

"Could the bubble have been a submarine's reconnaissance drone? Or was it something else?"

*Tiger Walking in Front of Safari Vehicle*

# 16. Shere Khan

*India*

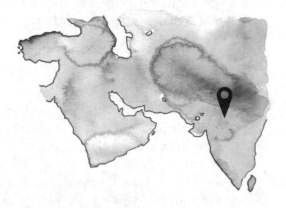

TIGERS HAVE A LONG HISTORY of preying on humans. When Britain ruled India, it kept meticulous track of tiger-caused deaths, counting about a thousand people killed by tigers annually. Even today, several dozen people are killed each year in India, usually during chance encounters in buffer zones around wildlife refuges. Indians in tiger country believe the beasts stalk and attack from behind. They often wear masks depicting human faces on the back of their heads, hoping to fool a stalking tiger.

One of the best places in the world to see tigers in the wild is Ranthambore National Park in India. Ranthambore is the living embodiment of Kipling's *Jungle Book*—giant trees, rolling hills, crocodile-filled lakes, and ancient temples.

## Scott's Story

I traveled to Ranthambore to see the tigers, staying in a tented camp on the edge of the park. I had been to Africa before, and the animals were easy to see on the plain. I'd soon learn that India was very different.

I awoke at 5 a.m. to start my first game drive. It was just me and my driver, heading into the jungle as the sun rose. The air was surprisingly cold—50 degrees in an open-air jeep. Bundled under a blanket, I asked my guide how often he sees a tiger.

"Every couple of days," he said.

"I'm here for seven days," I said.

"We will certainly see a tiger."

The jungle was thick, and it was hard to see the animals. Sightings were limited to the lakes and clearings, and occasionally animals walking on the road. There was an abundance of antelope, deer, and monkeys. I even saw a sloth bear.

"You have now seen all of the animals except the tiger," the guide said. "Now, we focus only on the tiger."

The basic approach to finding a tiger was to speed through the park, listening for alarm calls from monkeys. The monkeys alert each other to the presence of a tiger, similar to a dog barking. Every half hour or so, the jeep would come across alarm calls. We would stop, turn off the engine, and stare into the undergrowth, hoping to see a flash of orange.

The first drive ended without a tiger. We did the same thing again in the afternoon. And for the next five mornings and afternoons. Again and again there were alarm calls, but they always ended in disappointment. After six days of rough driving—bouncing around the jungle—I had yet to set eyes on a tiger.

On my second to last drive, I saw a crocodile lunge out of the lake and take down a giant antelope, pulling it into the water. The antelope fought valiantly, struggling to free itself. But other crocodiles came in and joined their brethren. Eventually, they pulled the beast under the water and drowned it.

"This is our lucky day," the guide said. "We will most definitely find a tiger."

He took me to a remote corner of the park to show me an ancient well. Stone steps led down at least two stories, to a square pool filled with spring water.

"That is an ancient spring," the driver said.

"Can I walk down there?" I asked.

The driver shook his head emphatically and said, "No. Not possible."

"Are you afraid of the invisible tiger?" I asked.

"I've seen what they can do," the guide said.

It was the perfect photo opportunity, and I didn't hear any alarm calls. "Let's walk down into the well and take a quick picture," I pleaded.

"Several years ago, I had a visitor who was bored—like you are now. We had been driving for days with no luck. I stopped when I heard the monkeys calling, and I was looking for the tiger. My guest was reading his book on the back bench of the jeep, his head down. He had given up on seeing a tiger.

"I heard no sound. Not even the rustle of a bush. All I saw out of the corner of my eye was a flash of orange movement. The beast leapt from the foliage and grabbed the man by the back of his neck, pulling him right off the jeep. Then it bounded again, with the man's body thrown over its back, like a rag doll—vanishing into the leaves.

"By the time I could grab my rifle, it was all over. The tiger was gone, sprinting into the jungle, its growing distance signaled by the gradually fading alarm calls. I radioed for the rangers, and trackers came. They gave chase, eventually finding the man's partially eaten body."

I was dumbfounded. I had always assumed these open safari vehicles were completely safe. I recalled being told in Africa that the lions viewed the vehicle as something large—and did not even realize there were people inside. The guide's story gave me goose bumps, and I decided against the walk.

We drove on until we heard alarm cries again. Before we came to a stop, my guide barked, "There is Shere Khan," and pointed to the right.

I followed his finger to a small clearing of tall grass. Standing still, about twenty yards distant, was the orange tiger, and it was staring right at us. Its stripes blended in with the grass, and but for the guide's expert eyes, I might have missed its presence. We followed the tiger for an hour, watching it stalk nearby antelope. When they spooked and ran off, the tiger walked slowly toward the road, coming within ten yards. It stopped walking and looked at us, or more precisely, at me. We locked eyes—one on one. I felt that the tiger recognized me as a human being, even though I was crouched down in the jeep. Then it went on its way, walking along the road, before slipping quietly into the forest.

A decade later, I saw an article about a man-eating tiger in Ranthambore. A tiger there named Ustad reportedly took four victims, including the assistant forest officer for the park. He also was famous for stalking and chasing jeeps. Unlike the tiger from my guide's story, he never took a tourist from a jeep. Nor did the story mention the fatality claimed by my guide.

It turns out that no such tourist fatality ever occurred at Ranthambore. The closest one came to death was in 2003 at Bandhavgarh National Park, when an injured tigress jumped into the back of a jeep and attacked two French tourists. The hotelier who was driving them jumped out and distracted the tiger by pulling her tail! The tigress fled and was never seen again. The two tourists were briefly hospitalized with cuts and bruises, and their driver received stitches. This event occurred just before my visit and was likely the inspiration for my guide's story. In hindsight, he was just trying to scare me enough so I wouldn't get out and walk down to the well. The unembellished version was frightening enough. It would have been sufficient to dissuade me.

# 17. The Fourth Girlfriend

*Lithuania*

WHEN THE SOVIET UNION COLLAPSED, it created tremendous opportunities for entrepreneurs to obtain ownership of government enterprises. Some succeeded through privatization, others by purchasing commodities at regulated, low domestic prices and then reselling them on the international market for profit. By 2004, *Forbes* magazine counted as many as thirty-six Russians who were billionaires. Many of them were remarkably young.

## Scott's Story

One of these tycoons (whom we will call Dmitri) was interested in my expertise in African oil and gas exploration, and invited me to meet with him in Vilnius. But this was not a typical business meeting in a conference room. It was a three-day social event, in which the bachelor Dmitri was celebrating the birthday of his girlfriend. He had invited me to join along in the festivities, promising to discuss business along the way.

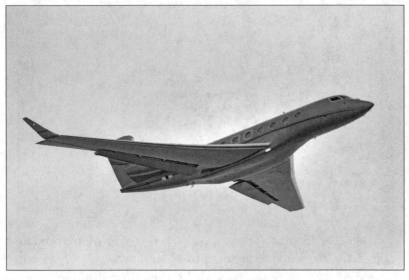

*Private Jet Landing in Moscow*

When we first met, Dmitri embraced me, as if we had been friends forever. He peppered me with questions about oil in Africa and my experience there. It was only later that I could pry his own story from him. When the Soviet Union collapsed, its communist government stopped paying miners. People were scared and hungry, and the mines often were abandoned altogether. Dmitri and his friends saw an opportunity amid the chaos. They sold everything they owned, borrowed whatever they could, and traveled to a mine near Dmitri's family home. Dmitri gathered the miners together, telling them that the world as they knew it was over—the Soviet Union was no more. If they wanted to eat, they needed to work for him.

Dmitri put the miners back to work. Over the following months, he sold the mine's production on the world market, rapidly growing his wealth. When the government finally got around to privatizing the mine, Dmitri and his friends were able to officially "buy" it—at a fraction of its real value.

At the first night's dinner, Dmitri sat me next to Elena, a student at the University of London. I learned far more about Dmitri sitting next to her than I did in my many meetings with him.

## The Fourth Girlfriend's Story

"I was having dinner with my girlfriends in London at a posh restaurant. That's where I caught Dmitri's eye. He had noticed me across the room. At the end of the evening, the waiter came over and said that our meal had been paid for by a gentleman—he pointed to Dmitri. He was older, but in great shape. I blew him a kiss in return, not expecting for it to lead anywhere.

"Before I could leave, one of his entourage came over and asked if I would like to join Dmitri for dessert. I was escorted to another table—for two. He was extraordinarily charming, asking me all about my classes and interests. I talked and talked, while he listened attentively. We were the last people there that night. He walked me to the street, where a Rolls Royce was waiting to take me home. Dmitri didn't even try to kiss my lips. He just shook my hand and then lifted it, kissing my fingers goodnight.

"The next day, Dmitri was waiting outside my classroom. He made me an offer, which was surprising. Dmitri wanted me to be his girlfriend—but there was a catch: I would only be his girlfriend for one week each month. There were three other girlfriends for the other weeks. 'All are treated equally,' he explained.

"I was offended. I remember feeling my face get hot with anger at the suggestion that this older man would not want me and me alone. But before I could reject his proposal, he kept calmly talking.

"'On the appointed week,' he said, 'one of my planes will bring you to me. I might be anywhere. Moscow, or my Mediterranean estate. You will stay with me for seven days and then be returned to London. Here, I will buy you an apartment—in your own name—which you can furnish as you wish. You will have one of my credit cards to buy anything you want.'

"I calmed myself down and told him that this was a lot to take in. I asked whether I might have a week to think about his proposal. He agreed and left. I shared the offer with my best friend, and we talked about it incessantly. The offer smacked of prostitution, but I really liked this man. There was something super-charming about Dmitri that drew me to him. He seemed to have read every book. He had something smart to say about anything and everything. He had a presence and confidence I had never experienced.

"The next week, Dmitri was waiting for me again outside my class. 'Have you had enough time to consider my offer?' he asked.

"'Would it be possible to accept on a trial basis, spending a week with you before either of us makes any further commitment?' I asked.

"He agreed, and the next month I boarded his plane and was whisked away to his villa in the south of France, near Nice. Dmitri's palace was perched on a hill, with expansive views over the azure Mediterranean. Terraced gardens of flowers and fruit trees descended toward the sea.

"The villa had the best of everything. Each bite of food was delicious. Then there was his entourage. Dmitri collected artists, writers, and musicians—well, just like he did women. I even recognized one of his guests, a well-known opera tenor. During the day, they painted and wrote and practiced. But at night, they belonged to Dmitri, filling the room with the most interesting conversations I had ever heard.

"After dinner, my head swimming with wine, Dmitri took me to his private quarters. He pressed a button, and the wall of glass facing the sea slid away, leaving his bedroom open to the night. We walked out onto the balcony. The lights of the coast and boats mingled with moonlight. I heard footsteps in the garden below. It was the tenor, carrying a bottle of wine. Then he started to sing, belting out an aria. I remember thinking that this must be what heaven is like.

"By the end of the week, I was in love with Dmitri. Of course, I accepted his offer. I believed that I would win his heart—that he would eventually be all mine. Two years later, I'm still waiting."

*Lion Eating a Giraffe*

# 18. The Dying Giraffe

## *South Africa*

ONE OF THE HIGHLIGHTS OF world travel is the African photo safari. The continent's best national parks are functioning ecosystems, preserved and protected from encroaching civilization. The animals roam free, as they have for millennia, in a never-ending chase of predator and prey.

Tourists pile into open Land Rovers and drive through the wilderness, watching the spectacle. The animals have become habituated to the presence of the vehicles, and they generally ignore them. As long as the tourists stay seated, the lions and leopards do not see them as prey. It all seems perfectly safe. . . until something goes wrong.

### The Game Driver's Story

"I was parked in a clearing with a family of four—mom, dad, and two small boys. Several giraffes wandered past our roofless

Land Rover, towering over us. One was a juvenile, much smaller than the rest. As my guests photographed them, a pride of lions rushed into the clearing. The lions came from every direction all at once, causing the giraffes to panic. The little one ran back toward the vehicle and was separated from its parents.

"A charging lioness lunged for the small giraffe, grabbing it near the base of its neck. Yet the giraffe kept on its feet, dragging the lion behind it—and heading right for us. In a flash, the distance between them and our Land Rover closed.

"I was expecting the giraffe to collapse before it reached us, or to turn and miss us, but the animal collided headlong into the side of the Rover. The two boys were in the last row of seats, and the parents were in the middle row. The giraffe's head and most of its neck careened forward, landing right between the parents and their boys, almost on the kids' laps. The lion was still outside the Rover, latched onto the giraffe, teeth sunk into the base of its neck.

"I grabbed my rifle and chambered a round, and yelled for everyone to stay down. Of course, no one listened to me. The parents were on their feet, reaching over the giraffe and trying to get the boys. As the boys screamed, the giraffe started to cough and gurgle. Then the blood poured from its mouth like a fountain. The dying animal writhed and twitched in agony, spraying blood all over the boys, soaking them.

"The Rover was now surrounded by approaching lions. I continued to yell for everyone to sit down and stay still—lest they attract the attention of one. I really wasn't sure what to do. I feared that if I tried to drive off, I would drag the giraffe, causing the lions to jump inside the vehicle. Then I started the vehicle, hoping its engine might scare them off. The lions were oblivious, though.

"A second lion leaped onto the back of the giraffe. Its weight pulled the giraffe free from the vehicle. No sooner than its head fell away, I sped off. We were driving downhill, and there was so much blood on the floor that it ran forward, soaking my boots. That afternoon, the family left early for Johannesburg. They had had enough of the African bush."

*The Sultan's Plane*

# 19. Smooth Air Decree

*Oman*

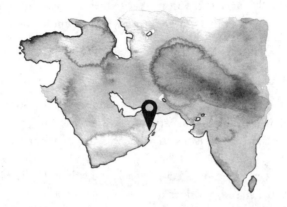

THE SULTANATE OF OMAN is on the southern Arabian Peninsula, facing the Indian Ocean. As its name implies, Oman is an absolute monarchy ruled by a Sultan. The current Sultan rose to power in 1970 by deposing his father in a palace coup, thereby becoming the fourteenth generation of his family to hold the throne. He remains childless, presumably so that none of his progeny can topple his reign.

Throughout Oman, it's hard to escape the Sultan. His portrait hangs everywhere, showing off his closely cropped white beard, paisley turban, and curved dagger, which he wears on his waist. Everything about his image evokes the most refined taste. His hobbies are no different. The Sultan's personal one hundred twenty-piece orchestra of Omani musicians plays for him at the palace, and his super yacht contains its own orchestra hall. When the Sultan travels, he does so in his flying palace—a Boeing 747 jumbo jet with the call sign "Oman One." The Sultan has other jets for his entourage, named, as you might imagine, "Oman Two," "Oman Three," and "Oman Four."

Scott spent several months negotiating petroleum agreements with the Sultanate. Although he never had the opportunity to personally meet the Sultan, Scott heard stories of palace life from members of his royal entourage. The most interesting of these concerned a secret decree.

## The Minister's Story

"One of the best things about being Sultan is the power to make instant law," the Minister explained. "If something is not to his liking, he simply banishes it. This was the case for the Smooth Air Decree.

"The Smooth Air Decree proclaimed that the flying palace, Oman One, shall no longer experience air turbulence. Like many of us, the Sultan is no fan of bouncing aircraft. Might the Sultan be afraid of turbulence? Certainly not! The Sultan fears nothing.

"The problem is a more delicate one. Oman One's entertainment system malfunctions when the plane experiences turbulence. That's because it consists of a string quartet—playing live. The Sultan's musicians often travel with him, playing their violins and cellos along the way. When the plane bounces, musicians miss their notes. String instruments require smooth air.

"How can any man control the skies, you may ask?

"Of course, storms can be seen on satellite images and radar. The Sultan's flight planners plot those and avoid them. The harder challenge is clear air turbulence. The Sultan's decree merely required a result. It did not specify how his servants would go about achieving it.

"On busy flyways, there are many planes heading in the same direction. Pilots often report air turbulence, enabling the later planes to avoid those altitudes. The solution arrived at by the Sultan's pilots was similar. They devised a system in which two smaller aircraft fly several minutes ahead of Oman One. One plane maintains the identical altitude of Oman One while the other flies higher or lower. If turbulence is experienced at Oman One's altitude, then the lead planes can search for smooth air. Once it is found, Oman One can be directed to ascend or descend to the clean air, thereby ensuring compliance with the Decree. The show must go on."

The *Wall Street Journal* interviewed several members of the Royal Oman Symphony Orchestra in 2001. Christopher Adey, chief conductor, explained that the ROSO is a "private court orchestra in a very European, ancient sense of the word." An Omani violinist echoed this sentiment, "We are first of all His Majesty's Orchestra; it was his idea, so we have to be good to him." A British instructor used to hearing applause at London concert halls even complained about the small royal audience: "Obviously, three or four people clapping can make only so much noise . . . so you do feel a bit dejected."

It's worth pausing to consider how far the Sultan has come. When he rose to power in 1970, his nation was among the poorest in the world, with only a few miles of paved streets and no secondary schools. Slavery was still legal. The Minister described how in his childhood, the gates of then-walled Muscat had to be locked at sunset to protect inhabitants from desert bandits—and how an oil rig making its way across the desert in the 1960s was attacked by camel-riding marauders shooting 19th-century muskets. Thanks to the Sultan, 21st-century Oman now has a growing middle class and ranks as one of the top 30 wealthiest nations in the world. Unlike other monarchs, maybe the Sultan has earned his personal orchestra, his 747, and . . . smooth air.

*Luanda, Angola*

# 20. Evicted

*Angola*

AFTER THE ANGOLAN CIVIL WAR ENDED, its capital, Luanda, became a boomtown. Boarded-up storefronts were transformed into swanky boutiques and restaurants. The one problem facing travelers was a shortage of hotel rooms. There were only two functioning hotels—the Alvalade and the Tropico—and many of their rooms were permanently booked year-round by oil companies. The few that remained required weeks-in-advance reservations. Yet the Angolan national oil company often summoned its partners to negotiations on short notice. Such invitations left oil men scrambling to procure rooms.

## Scott's Story

There were two of us on the Angola negotiating team, myself and a young Californian who had never traveled beyond the United States and Europe. Mr. California was already nervous about his first trip to Africa, peppering me with questions about obscure diseases I had never even heard of. When we were unable to secure rooms at either hotel, the oil minister offered up a better solution—the President of Angola's personal guesthouse.

Upon our arrival, we were taken to a gated mansion overlooking the Atlantic Ocean. It had butlers, a chef, and a swimming pool. The Californian smiled when we were greeted with glasses of champagne.

"This is nicer than any hotel I've ever stayed at!" he exclaimed. "I can't believe I was so worried about coming here."

We enjoyed two nights of pampered luxury at the hands of the President's staff. Dinners were an epicurean affair of grilled lobsters and fine wines. Little did we know, it was all about to come to an end.

The next day we pulled up to the guardhouse, but the gate did not open. As our driver argued with the guard in Portuguese, the butler arrived with our suitcases.

"Are those our bags?" Mr. California asked.

We got out of the vehicle and walked over to the English-speaking butler to find out what was going on.

"Portugal's Minister of Finance is scheduled to arrive at any minute," he said sheepishly, unable to look either of us in the eye.

"Where are we supposed to go?" I asked.

"A hotel?" he replied.

"The reason we're staying here is because the hotels are sold out."

The butler shrugged and handed us our suitcases.

We had just been evicted on order of the President of Angola.

"What do we do?" Mr. California asked.

"Let's try the hotels again," I said.

We visited each, and the result was the same. There were no rooms at any price.

As darkness started to fall, I recalled an acquaintance who owned a local construction company. I phoned him in the United States. He explained that his company leased a private home, which it used as a dormitory for employees.

"There's no guarantee they have space for you," he cautioned, "but I'll give them a ring now to let them know you are coming over."

By the time we reached the villa, it was dark. The general manager greeted us with Coca-Colas.

"Look," he said, "all of the bedrooms here are fully occupied. The only spaces we have are two servant's rooms in the backyard. They are pretty rough—no air conditioning—but each has a bed and a cold shower. Would you like to have a look?"

The rooms were worse than I had imagined, each with an open window and torn-up insect screen. The mattresses were bare and soiled, splattered with rodent droppings.

"I'd rather sleep in the car," Mr. California said.

"I'm pretty sure your driver has gone home to his family for the night," said the general manager. "Anyway, you'd be robbed if you tried to sleep in a car on these mean streets.

"This isn't the Holiday Inn, but it's safe. This compound has a ten-foot-tall razor wire fence and two armed guards. There's nothing to be concerned about."

Mr. California went to his quarters, and I, to mine. When I turned on the lights, bugs immediately started flying in through the broken window. I quickly switched them off and stretched a t-shirt over the bars, creating a makeshift bug screen.

Then there was the matter of the twin mattress. It was filthy, and there were no sheets. I dusted it off as best I could, put on a pair of jeans, and went to sleep in my clothes. Before I knew it, my alarm clock was going off.

*That wasn't so bad.*

I took a cold shower, put on my suit, and then walked outside, reasonably rested and ready for another day of negotiations. Mr. California was already waiting for me, suitcase in hand. His pale white face was covered in red bumps, and he looked like he had chicken pox.

"Mosquitoes," he said, pointing at his face. "I can't stay here another night. I've already tried to book a flight, but it looks like everything is sold out."

"Let's see what we can do," I said.

When we arrived at the negotiations, it turned out that our Angolan hosts were unaware that we had been evicted from the President's guest house. One arm of the government had no idea what the other one was doing. They made a few calls and proclaimed the problem solved. There was a nearly finished apartment complex where we could stay.

After the negotiations concluded, our driver took us to a midrise apartment building that was still surrounded by a construction fence. A foreman wearing a hard hat—who spoke broken English—greeted us at the gate and walked us through a maze of equipment to a working elevator.

He took us to the penthouse, a three-bedroom luxury apartment fully furnished with appliances and a big screen TV. The foreman showed us the brand-new mattresses and pillows, which still had plastic on them. There were unopened sets of sheets, too. The only things missing were light fixtures. Exposed wires dangled from the ceiling where they would soon be installed.

I turned to the foreman and said, "Thank you."

"One thousand dollars," he replied, holding out his hand.

That wasn't quite the "you're welcome" I was expecting, but I reached into my briefcase and gladly paid his asking price. We were so happy to have a nice place to sleep that we didn't even try to negotiate.

# 21. The Floating Islands

*Peru*

LAKE TITICACA IS LOCATED in the Andes Mountains at an elevation of more than 12,500 feet. It's the highest navigable lake in the world. Not far from its shores, in neighboring Bolivia, are the ruins of Tiahuanaco, one of the earliest civilizations in the Andes. Its ruins date back to 1500 BC and include a collection of stone faces lining the walls of a temple. What's most striking about the faces is that they appear to represent ethnic groups from around the world—Africans, Asians, and Europeans—from a time when, presumably, the people of Tiahuanaco had no contact with these distant peoples. Around the year 1,000 AD, a brutal drought hit the high Andes, leading Tiahuanaco's residents to abandon their city. What happened to them? One theory is that the modern-day descendants of Tiahuanaco live on today—as the Uros people. The Uros reside on self-constructed "floating islands" in the middle of Lake Titicaca.

*Mysterious Faces of Tiahuanaco*

## Gina's Story

As our small boat puttered across the lake toward the floating islands, we caught our first glimpses of the Uros. We watched dozens of men wading chest deep in the reed fields. I reached down and touched the water. It was frigid.

"That's cold!" I said.

"Not to them," our guide replied. "The Uros claim to have 'black blood,' which makes them immune from the lake's cold waters."

"What are they doing?" Scott asked.

"Most of them are harvesting reeds," said our guide. "Thousands of those reeds are woven together to create a foundation for each floating island. The more reeds, the more weight an island can support. The islands have preserved the Uros culture by limiting their contact with the rest of the world—including invading Incas and Spaniards."

Our guide had arranged a visit to one of the sixty floating islands. Stepping out onto the island was like walking on a sponge. The reeds crunched and gave way beneath each footfall, then sprang back as weight was released.

The Uros family, including a four-year-old boy, demonstrated how they harvest reeds and build their islands. Looking around, I realized that the islands have no railings. A child could easily fall into the water and drown.

"How do the children know to stay away from the water?" I asked.

Our guide translated our question and their answer. "Within these waters live giant frogs. They lurk around the edges of the islands, waiting for a child to get close to the edge. Then they shoot their long, sticky tongues out of the water to grab the child. This is the first story every child hears. Because no child wants to get eaten by a frog, boys and girls stay away from the edge. The tale of the child-eating frogs protects them from drowning."

"Can you please ask them what's the strangest thing they have ever seen living on the lake?" Scott asked.

Our guide conversed with the Uros family for a few minutes and then resumed his translation. "Six families live on this island now, but it used to house seven. Because the reeds at the bottom of the islands are constantly rotting, new reeds must be added to the surface, or floor, every few months. Each family is expected to contribute to the work needed to maintain their shared island. Laziness is not tolerated. Everyone has to pull his or her own weight. But the seventh family refused to harvest reeds. In the middle of the night, while they slept, the other families took saws and began cutting away the portion of the island on which the lazy family lived. Eventually, it broke off and floated away. The family then had to maintain their small island entirely on their own—before another group eventually allowed them to join. They learned their lesson. Now they work to maintain their new island."

The visit concluded with the Uros family taking us on a tour of the village in their ceremonial reed boat. It was a catamaran, with two parallel hulls that supported a two-story center console. The front hulls curved upwards, with each bow forming the head of a puma. Rowers propelled us silently across the lake.

As we paddled along, I gazed upward at the cloudless sky. It looked different from other skies. It was a darker, deeper blue. The sky's color was so similar to the lake's that one appeared to be a mirror image of the other. On the horizon, the blue of the two merged seamlessly together. Was the sky reflecting the water, or was the water reflecting the sky?

# 22. The First Hmong Lawyer in Laos

*Laos*

APPROXIMATELY HALF A MILLION Hmong people live in northern Laos. During the Vietnam War, the Hmong aligned themselves with the United States and to this day they remain fiercely anti-communist and independent. Unfortunately for the Hmong, Laos remains a one-party socialist nation that continues to espouse the philosophies of Marx and Lenin. While most of the Hmong have been subdued by the government, a few thousand—the Hmong ChaoFa—still fight on from their jungle hideouts.

We were introduced to the Hmong culture by Yah (pronounced like the cheer Americans give their sports team) in Luang Prabang, Laos. He took us on winding roads through the mountains to a Hmong village. We brought pencils and paper to the elementary school and then were allowed to watch a shaman undertake a healing ceremony. The shaman wore a hood and

*Red Centipede*

balanced on a wooden bench while his assistants sacrificed a pig. Even more interesting was Yah's personal story.

## Yah's Story

"My grandfather just celebrated his 104th birthday. He worked for the CIA during the Vietnam War and received a letter granting him safe passage to the United States. All he needed to do was make it to the designated refugee camp in Thailand. Unfortunately, communist soldiers identified him at the ferry crossing, and he had to dive into the Mekong River. He swam as fast as he could as bullets splashed all around him. While he managed to escape, his letter and passport were washed away. He made it to the refugee camp, but they turned him away. He had lost his chance to become an American and had no choice but to return to our mountain village. That's where I grew up.

"Because we Hmong were on the wrong side of the war, the communist government provided us with little support. The nearest elementary school was a two-hour walk through the jungle of a national park. I had no shoes, either. Each morning, I rose at dawn and marched bare-footed through the darkness. I was scared of the animals. There were still tigers then, but fortunately I never saw one. I did step on giant centipedes seven times, though. To this day, I know how many I stepped on because their bites were so painful.

"The worst days, though, were the two times I was bitten on the hand by a tree viper. My parents had to bring the shaman to our hut to save my life. There are certain hawks that eat vipers as part of their diet. The shaman made me drink a tea made of the ground remains of these hawk's talons—which were believed to hold a kind of anti-venom. It did seem to work, and I eventually recovered.

"Most of the other students in my village gave up on school. I was one of the few that kept walking the four-hour round trip. But when elementary school was over, there was no other school I could walk to. To continue my education, I would have to go away to boarding school, something my family could not afford.

"When I was eleven, they put me to work on their poppy farm. It wasn't for me, though. I had learned enough from my grandfather's stories to know that my destiny lay elsewhere. So, I ran away to the village where the school was and stowed away in the back of a truck heading south. When it stopped, I found myself in Luang Prabang.

"I was hungry and scared. Smelling food, I approached a Buddhist monastery. The monks took me in. Even better, they also ran a school. I was able to work in exchange for continuing my education.

"Buddhism was both familiar and strange to me. We Hmong are spirit worshippers and believe that each person has multiple spirits. When we die, one of our souls is reborn as another's body, similar to Buddhism's reincarnation, another stays behind to watch over its family, and yet another continues on to live in the spirit world, similar to your heaven.

"After I learned everything they had to teach, the monks thought I should go on to the university in Laos's capital. They found me a scholarship, and that paid for my first couple of years. Unfortunately, the scholarship ran out, and I had to start paying my own way. I needed to work on the weekend—so that I could go to school during the week. I found a job at a rock quarry that paid $5 per ton of rock hauled up to a barge waiting on the Mekong River. On a good day, I managed four tons over eighteen hours of work. It paid off, though. Those rocks put me through college and law school, where I finished in the top 10 percent on the Laos bar exam. That's how I became the first Hmong lawyer in Laos."

# 23. A Pug in Peril

*Saudi Arabia*

THE ISLAMIC FAITHFUL FEEL very strongly about pigs. Books celebrating the porcine, such as *Animal Farm* and *Charlotte's Web*, have been banned in certain nations due to their depictions of pigs. English dictionaries even sometimes have the word "pig" blacked out with a marker.

Saudi Arabia is particularly sensitive. As the host nation of the Holy Mosque of Mecca, Saudi Arabia bans pork and pigs altogether. Their very presence within the nation is considered a desecration. For this reason, some Saudi citizens may not even know what a pig looks like.

An acquaintance was in the process of moving from the United Arab Emirates to Saudi Arabia when he was stopped at the border for a routine search of his vehicle. Accompanying him was his dog. Although legal, dogs also are uncommon in Saudi Arabia because they are viewed as impure or unclean animals.

*Pug or Pig?*

## The Pug Owner's Story

"The Saudi border police are notoriously strict enforcers of the nation's religious laws, so I was careful to ensure nothing in my vehicle would run afoul of their rules. The only thing I was worried about was my dog, a cute little pug. I had all of his veterinarian records and health certifications with me and was ready to present them if asked.

"When the Saudi guard approached, I rolled down my window, and he leaned in for a closer look at my passenger cabin.

"'What's that?' he asked, pointing to my pug sitting beside me on the front passenger seat.

"'It's my pug,' I casually replied.

"This elicited a look of complete disgust. The officer backed away from the vehicle, putting his white-gloved hand over his mouth.

"The guard blew his whistle, and three more guards—these with machine guns at their sides—surrounded my car. They were talking rapidly in Arabic, and I couldn't make out their concern.

"'Get out!' shouted one of them.

"It was a scorching hot day in the Arabian desert, and I couldn't leave my pug in the car. I reached over to pick him up—

"'Leave the pig!' barked the guard.

"Unfortunately, I had not thought about how a pug might resemble a pig. It has a curly tail, not unlike a pig's tail, and a stubby round nose—well, rather similar to a pig's snout. And to someone less accustomed to the English language, one might hear the word pug as pig.

"I let go of my pug and stepped out of the vehicle, smiling and hoping to quickly resolve the case of mistaken identity.

"'It's not a P-I-G, it's a P-U-G, which is a kind of dog. You know, *woof woof*.'

"That led to a blank stare. I didn't think I had gotten through to him. By now, the commotion had attracted other Saudis, who were leaving their vehicles to see what was the matter. They gathered around to look at the pug, each recoiling in horror. My poor pug was panting and drooling in the 115-degree heat.

"The guards chattered away in Arabic and then one said, 'We kill the pig. Take it over there.' The guard pointed to the desert alongside the road.

"'It's not a pig!' I shouted. 'It's a dog.'

"The youngest guard was putting on latex gloves, apparently in preparation for my pug's execution. Just when I thought all was lost, my pug was rescued by a good Samaritan. An older Saudi man intervened, explaining to the guard that my animal was, in fact, a species of dog—not a pig. They talked for some time, but a reprieve was eventually won. We were allowed to go on our way, and my pug was no longer a pig."

# 24. The Accidental Masseur

*Madagascar*

A CALIFORNIA-SIZED PIECE OF AFRICA lies by itself in the southern Indian Ocean, about five hundred miles from the mainland. If you drew a line from San Diego straight through the center of the earth, it would emerge near Madagascar. The furthest distance between any two points on the planet, or antipode, is a little more than twelve thousand miles. Madagascar lies more than eleven thousand miles away from the American West Coast.

To call Madagascar "African" is a stretch. It separated from Africa millions of years ago, and its flora, fauna, and people are unique. Madagascar has snakes, but they have no venom. Then there are the lemurs, thirty-three species in all, which exist nowhere else in the world. Until the 18th century, Madagascar also was home to the largest bird in the world, the Elephant Bird. It stood more than ten feet tall and weighed one thousand pounds. Its eggs were bigger than footballs.

*Baobab Trees in Madagascar*

## Scott's Story

My company had acquired the right to explore for oil off the coast of northwest Madagascar. I flew to Madagascar's capital, Antananarivo, to meet with the oil minister and other officials. When those meetings concluded, I chartered a small plane and headed to the oil concession—Anjajavy. I was interested in seeing the impact of a newly opened resort by a national park—an ancient forest of baobabs and rosewood trees filled with lemurs. The resort introduced modernity not only to the region's wildlife, but also to a nearby fishing village. Until the resort's arrival, they had lived off the land and sea. I was wondering how they had reacted to a five-star hotel in their midst and a constant stream of millionaires trekking through their wilderness.

I sat in the front seat of a Cessna with my pilot as we flew two hours across Madagascar. The sky here was so quiet that we never encountered another plane. In fact, my pilot spent most of the flight reading the newspaper. We landed on a red dirt airstrip, and were met by one of the hotel's new Land Rovers. The resort itself was another half hour drive. My first impression was that they had done a nice job. It was a collection of thatched huts strung along a crescent of white sand looking out on the turquoise Indian Ocean. It all blended quite seamlessly into the landscape.

Over the course of my stay there, I learned that most of the hotel's employees were locals, hired from the nearby fishing village. This was even the case for the masseur, a young man whose face was affixed with a permanent smile. I was out on my veranda early one morning talking on my satellite phone while the masseur was giving a massage to a woman staying at a neighboring villa. My call finished just as he walked by.

"Good morning," I said. "Can I ask you a question?"

"Sure," he said, bounding up to my villa.

"I heard you were from the Anjajavy village."

"Yes," he said.

"Did you have any prior training as a masseur?"

"No," he replied. "The resort trained me."

"How did you know you wanted to me a masseur?"

"The hotel manager came to my village, offering employment. No skills were needed. Everyone would be trained by the resort. The hotel manager then invited everyone who was interested in working at the resort to form a single file line. I joined the line out of curiosity—mostly about what jobs there would be and how much money I might make. At the front of the line, the manager held a basket. Everyone was instructed to draw a single card from the basket. We were told that each card had the name of a job—receptionist, maid, driver, guide, waiter, bellman, gardener, cook, and, of course, masseur."

The young man then smiled even more broadly. "I drew the luckiest card."

"What happened next?" I asked.

"I was told what my wages would be. They were more than I could have imagined. Even better, they would send me to a massage therapist school in Paris. It was like a dream."

"And here you are. Do you enjoy your profession?" I asked.

He smiled broadly. "I do."

"What would your life have been like if the hotel had never come here?" I asked.

"Before I drew the lucky card, I had dreamed of being a physician. I did well in school and had won a scholarship to college in the capital."

"That sounds like a great opportunity, too. Why did you choose to work for the hotel rather than become a doctor?"

"There is a saying you English have: 'a bird in the hand is better than many in the bushes.' That's how I felt. The wages being offered by the hotel were big. The massage school was only a few months. For the other, it would have taken many years to become a doctor. Who knows whether I would have made it? I also would have been away from my family. Now, I'm successful—living in paradise here, with my own people."

I have often thought about the young masseur, and how the European resort had so dramatically altered the course of his life. When industries come to places like Anjajavy, offering high wages, the practical result is that they divert people from what they otherwise would have done. Maybe that's better for them. Maybe not. The masseur has good work. He even enjoys it. But what happens if the hotel closes? Where does he find work? Would it be too late to become a doctor?

The ultimate effect of travel is never clear. But for the time being, at least, the masseur seemed an example of travel's positive impact.

*Abbottabad, Pakistan*

# 25. Hello, Mr. Bin Laden

*Pakistan*

EARLY 2002 WAS A DIFFICULT TIME for Pakistan, with the war against Al-Qaeda raging next door in Afghanistan. The most wanted man in the world, Osama bin Laden, had escaped the Americans at the Battle of Tora Bora, on the Afghanistan-Pakistan border, by fleeing into northwest Pakistan. In January of 2002, one of bin Laden's lieutenants had kidnapped and executed an American reporter for the *Wall Street Journal*. Two months later, they had bombed a church full of diplomats in Islamabad, killing five and wounding 40. It was against this backdrop that Pakistan held an auction to privatize several oil fields.

## Scott's Story

My employer wanted to buy the Pakistani oil fields. Companies wishing to participate in government auctions send an executive from the home office who has the authority to bid hundreds of millions of dollars. It might have been that everyone else was otherwise occupied that week. Or maybe they were scared to travel to Islamabad in the midst of so much violence. Whatever the case, the job fell to me, a 32-year-old who had been at the company for less than six months.

I was young and fearless then, so it was all fine by me. My plane arrived at the Islamabad airport in the middle of the night, and I was met with an armed security detail of a driver and two guards with machine guns. As we made our way out of the airport, I asked the guard riding in the back seat with me what was the strangest thing he had seen in Islamabad.

"Look around at all the bikes and pedestrians—even at four in the morning."

Sure enough, they were everywhere, dodging traffic.

"Mostly, these are poor people. They are walking or riding a rickety bike because they cannot even afford a bus. When one of them is struck, the vehicle just keeps going. It doesn't stop. If the cyclist or pedestrian is still alive, bystanders may render aid, or call for an ambulance. If the person is dead, though, it's not unusual for the body to just be left on the side of the road. There is one nearby. Three days have passed. Still there. We are coming up to the body now."

The guard directed the driver to pull over on the side of the road. As he did, the headlights shone down into a drainage ditch. Illuminated in front of them was the naked body of a man, lying face down on the edge of a flooded ditch. The upper torso was in the water, with its arms and hands extended and floating, while the rest of him lay upon the embankment.

"Where are his clothes?" I asked.

"Stolen. Within minutes of his death, others had taken everything on him. When I first saw him, he was already stripped bare."

I felt sad for this man, whose life had been prematurely taken in a tragic accident. I wondered whether his relatives were out looking for him. Surely, he was someone's son, or husband, or father. How could the government just leave him there—wasn't there a morgue?

Not ten minutes from the body, we reached a security checkpoint on the outskirts of Islamabad. Several soldiers wearing helmets peered out from sandbag bunkers on both sides of the road—pointing their machine guns in our direction. Two of them cautiously approached our vehicle. One asked for our passports while the other looked under the vehicle with a mirror attached to a pole. They even opened the trunk and rummaged through my suitcase.

"The capital is a secure area," my guard said.

When we reached the Islamabad Marriott Hotel, we encountered yet another security check. Before we could enter the driveway, armed guards checked my name against the hotel's guest list and again looked under the land cruiser with mirrors. Climbing out of the car, I was met by more armed guards who were operating an x-ray machine and metal detector, indistinguishable from an airport security checkpoint. Even though I did not set off the metal detector, a guard on the other side quickly patted me down. This was all before I had even reached the hotel's front desk.

After I had checked in, my guard pulled me aside. "You are in a rear-facing room, overlooking the pool," he said. "Please keep the curtains drawn at all times. That will minimize flying glass in the event of a bombing."

While my stay at the Marriott was uneventful, six years later a suicide bomber attacked the hotel with a car bomb, killing 54 and injuring another 266. The bombing was graphically depicted in the 2012 movie *Zero Dark Thirty*, which chronicled the capture of Osama bin Laden.

The petroleum auction was a success, with my bid prevailing. As the winning bidder, though, I had to stay for further negotiations. Sometimes a day or two would pass between meetings. On these days, my security detail wanted to keep me moving. Each morning, we drove out away from Islamabad in a different direction. The second driving day, we headed into the Northwest Frontier Province with the goal of trying to catch a distant glimpse of Pakistan's tallest mountain, K2. The first town we passed through was called Abbottabad. There, I posed for a picture with a bearded man who kept a pet eagle on his shoulder. When I returned to the land cruiser, all of the guards were laughing.

"What's so funny?" I asked.

"The eagle man is a dead ringer for Osama bin Laden!" the guard said.

I looked back at him, and sure enough, they could have been twins.

"Remember, there's a $20 million reward," he joked.

About a decade later, the hunt for bin Laden eventually came to an end right there. The bin Laden hideout was a short walk of a few hundred yards from where I had posed with Osama's doppelgänger.

# 26. Prehistoric Forest

*Seychelles Islands*

THE SEYCHELLES ARE AN ARCHIPELAGO of one hundred fifteen islands located in the middle of the Indian Ocean. Of these, forty-five are granite, the remnants of a lost continent that was ripped apart and sunk by plate tectonics millions of years ago. These ancient mountaintops are home to lost species, including the largest tortoises in the world and many unique plants.

## Gina's Story

We were in the Seychelles on business—presenting a proposal to the Minister of Finance for how the nation could explore for oil and gas in its waters. While the Seychelles have no oil or gas wells, oil continues to wash ashore on its beaches. The oil is believed to be seeping out of the Indian Ocean seafloor, finding its way from an oil field buried within the sunken continent. While at dinner

*Seychelles Beach*

with the Minister of Finance and his wife, I asked him what was the strangest thing on their islands.

The Minister described a magical forest of giant palm trees within a secluded valley on the island of Praslin.

"The fossil records show that the earth was once dominated by these palm trees," the Minister said. "It's the same forest the dinosaurs lived in sixty-five million years ago. Giant palm trees thrived then, but as the air changed, conifers and deciduous trees out-competed the palms across the planet. But the remnant population here was free from these competitors. They are living fossils."

"The most amazing palm is the Coco de Mer," said his wife. "The tallest recorded was one hundred eighty-six feet high. Each leaf is twenty feet long and twelve feet wide, and its fruit is the largest nut in the world."

"The nut takes almost seven years to mature," explained the Minister, "eventually weighing thirty-five pounds and having a diameter of one and a half feet."

"You have to go there," the Minister's wife urged.

The next day we went to the airport and flew to Praslin Island, hiking off into the Vallée de Mai.

The Minister and his wife were right. It felt like stepping into another world. The giant trees and their leaves dwarfed us. So, too, were the palm leaves and trunks strangely shaped. The differences were not merely visual, either. The leaves made spooky rustling sounds as the sea breeze blew through the valley. The forest smelled funny, too. We were walking through a valley of living fossils. As the winds picked up, we kept an eye skyward, wary of the possibility that one of the giant nuts might come crashing down.

When we finished our hike, we visited the park's museum, which had several nuts for sale. Some were bigger than basketballs. While we examined one, the curator approached.

"Where are you from?" he asked.

"America," I said.

He was clearly surprised. "Not many Americans make it here. It's good that you saw it now, though. In another couple of decades, this all may be gone."

"They've survived sixty-five million years. Why are they threatened now?" I asked.

"The Coco de Mer is suffering the same fate as the rhinoceros. The kernel inside the Coco de Mer nut is a pricy aphrodisiac in Asia because when held a certain way, it looks like a woman's rear end—albeit some imagination is required. Traders pay $200 a pound for it, which means one nut can fetch $7,000. Over time, poachers have taken so many from the forest that there are no longer enough young trees to replace the dying ones. Even worse, once a poacher cuts a seed, the palm is damaged and can no longer generate as many seeds as before."

The Coco de Mer nut and the rhinoceros horn are both victims of their passing resemblance to human fertility. Unfortunately, over the last few decades, technology has enabled the more efficient harvesting of endangered species. It's cheaper to travel to exotic destinations. More travel and trade between nations have also made it easier for smugglers to blend in with legitimate traffic and sneak their products by customs agents. Our visit to Praslin's prehistoric forest reminded us that efforts to preserve our planet's natural heritage are more challenging—and more critical—than ever before.

# 27. Too Close for Comfort

*Rwanda*

THE VIRUNGA LODGE SITS atop a hill, looking toward the peaks of eight volcanoes in Rwanda, Uganda, and the Democratic Republic of Congo. At night, guests sip wine on the lodge's porch, watching the volcanoes erupt fireworks in the distance. During the day, they climb these same peaks in search of ancient primates—golden monkeys and mountain gorillas. Armed guards walk in front of them, hacking away with machetes at ten-foot-high tangles of stinging nettles.

The primates move freely around their home ranges, shadowed by their own guards to protect them from poachers. To reach them requires climbing for hours up the steep slopes, slipping and sliding through muddy ash flows. The ultimate prize is the opportunity to spend an hour in the company of a mountain gorilla family. The mountain gorillas are so genetically similar to humans that they are vulnerable to our illnesses. Visitors undergo health exams before each trek to ensure they do not introduce contagions.

*Volcanoes National Park, Rwanda*

Trekkers are carefully instructed on how to act around the giant apes. Do not point at them, as doing so might be mistaken for the motion of a spear thrower. Avoid direct eye contact, as this could be viewed as challenging them. Of course, guests also are not permitted to touch the beasts. It seems impossible that a mountain gorilla would allow a human being to reach out and touch it. Yet that's exactly what these gentle giants would let you do.

## Gina's Story

After hours of crawling through a steep, muddy forest of stinging nettles, we finally found our gorilla family. They were eating lunch in a bamboo grove—two dozen of them, in all shapes and sizes. They were breaking, peeling, and chewing bamboo. Such a fearsome creature—the inspiration for King Kong—is actually a vegetarian. That's what makes this interaction so extraordinary. You can't sit on the savannah with a pride of lions. They'll eat you.

I had imagined that all gorillas would look alike. Yet being so close, I realized that each was unique in its body shape and face—just like human beings. They acknowledged our arrival, looking us up and down with their big eyes. But then it was back to chewing on the bamboo.

There were babies, too, or more aptly, gorilla toddlers. They were playing with each other, tumbling around their mothers' feet. At one point, a baby gorilla ran right across my boots as it was being chased by another.

The giant patriarch—a very buff silverback—was the only stern-looking one in the bunch. He kept a watchful eye over us. As rays of sunlight played on his rippling muscles, I recalled the joke, "Where does an eight hundred-pound gorilla sit? Anywhere it wants to." When the silverback decided to walk through the middle of our group, the guide warned everyone to get out of his way. A minor panic ensued among us, a primal example of every man for himself. Scott and other guests bumped into me as we tried to escape, and I fell backwards into a wall of bamboo. They all left me there to face the silverback alone. The giant sauntered by, just a few feet away. As he looked over at me, I remembered the rule about not making eye contact, and quickly averted my eyes toward the ground. He passed by without incident.

On the way back down the mountain, I asked our guide what was the strangest thing he had ever seen while visiting the gorillas.

"Do you remember how we warned you not to point at the gorillas?" he asked.

"Yes, because they might think we are throwing a spear at them."

"Last year, a visitor became so excited upon seeing the silver-back that he broke the cardinal rule. This drew the silverback's alarmed stare. Do you remember the second rule?"

"Don't lock eyes with them," I said.

"He then broke the second rule—and stared right back at the silverback. In an instant, the silverback was upon the man. The great ape grabbed my guest by his calf, upending him. Then the giant ran off into the undergrowth, dragging the poor man behind, right up the side of the volcano.

"It all happened so fast. I gave chase, but it was no use. My visitor's screams got softer and softer until they seemed to be very far away. I stayed with the others while the trackers followed the drag path, hacking their way along until they finally recovered the man. He had been abandoned by the silverback a few hundred yards away.

"How badly was he injured?" I asked.

"He managed to escape any serious injuries—just a few scrapes and bruises and nettle stings."

Mountain gorillas face an uncertain future. Poachers hunt them for their meat, which has become a prestigious delicacy among Africa's elites. The greater threat, though, appears to be a loss of their habitat. A horizontal line is visible on the side of the volcano. It is the advance of deforestation, driven both by agriculture and the need for charcoal fuel.

We visited a charcoal-maker and watched how he transformed giant trees from the mountain into household fuel. Whether the gorillas survive depends on stopping people like the charcoal-maker. The Rwanda government recently raised ticket prices to trek to the gorillas to $1,500 per person, per day. It plans to use the funds to help the surrounding communities transition to more sustainable practices. For example, solar panels can be used instead of charcoal. Locals also have been recruited to be on the watch for poachers. These efforts appear to be working. The population of mountain gorillas in the Virunga mountains has increased by more than one hundred—to about six hundred gorillas—so far this decade.

*Jost Van Dyke Island*

# 28. Lord of the Flies

*British Virgin Islands*

THE BRITISH VIRGIN ISLANDS ARE a sailors' paradise of more than fifty islands in the Caribbean Sea. Jost Van Dyke is one of their favorites. This island once produced sugar and cotton, but now its main industry is tourism. It hosts nearly seven thousand boats per year, and thousands of partiers converge on the island for its "Old Year's Night" party each New Year's Eve.

Among Jost Van Dyke's famous bars is the Soggy Dollar Bar, birthplace of the Painkiller—a potent concoction of Pusser's Rum, pineapple juice, orange juice, cream of coconut, and fresh nutmeg. The bar's name comes from the fact that there is no dock. Boats drop anchor in the bay, and then everyone has to swim in to shore. This, of course, means that Painkillers and other cocktails are usually paid for with, well, wet dollar bills.

## Gina's Story

We dropped anchor at lunchtime and swam to shore for a bite to eat at the Soggy Dollar. Its tables and surrounding beach were packed with intoxicated boaters downing one Painkiller after another. After about fifteen minutes of hunting for a table, we finally found one.

I like clean, and the Soggy Dollar Bar was not up to my usual standards. We stood in line to order, and I opted for something simple—a kid's grilled cheese. How could that go wrong? Scott chose the fish and chips.

We people-watched while waiting for our food. Most everyone around us was intoxicated and twenty years our junior. It reminded me of Spring Break.

"Here comes our lunch," Scott said, seeing our waitress carrying a tray in our direction.

As she worked her way through the crowd, I noticed that diners were swatting at something in the air as she passed by them.

"Are those insects?" I asked.

"Where?" Scott said.

"Chasing our waitress."

The answer came as the waitress deposited our food in front of us. A swarm of hundreds of giant flies, most a shiny green color, were in pursuit of our lunch. They were landing all over me, and I was swatting away at them without effect.

"Let's eat quickly," Scott said, cutting into a filet of steaming fried fish.

Before he could fork his first piece, dozens of flies landed and crawled into and underneath the fish batter. One after another, more landed, until the batter coating moved up and down with the crawling of flies beneath it.

Scott looked so pathetic. He was holding his fork in the air over his fish, frozen, with his mouth open.

Fortunately, I was fast enough to cover my grilled cheese with a napkin before any flies could descend on it.

"Let's abandon your fish and head to the beach," I said.

I grabbed my food, and we made our escape. The flies, happy to have captured Scott's fish, did not follow. We found a nice hard patch of sand on the surf's edge and sat down. I divided my toasted cheese and gave half to Scott. I ate my one-half of a cheese sandwich, while trying not to think about how many flies might be inhabiting the Soggy Dollar's kitchen.

The novel *Lord of the Flies* is set on a beautiful, tropical island, albeit one inhabited by flies. Its name comes from a scene in which a boy happens on the fly-covered remains of a pig. The flies proceed to land on the boy and crawl all over him. As I swam back to our boat, I thought about those flies. Just as in the novel, the flies on our island were "black and iridescent green and without number."

*Nouakchott, Mauritania*

# 29. Digging Your Own Grave

*Mauritania*

NOUAKCHOTT, THE CAPITAL OF MAURITANIA, lies sandwiched between the encroaching sands of the Sahara Desert and the Atlantic Ocean. It's hot, dry, dusty, and prone to plagues. Swarms of locusts periodically blacken its skies, devouring leaves. Giant fruit bats—resembling foxes with wings—also descend upon the capital by the thousands, feasting on fruits such as dates.

On August 3, 2005, Mauritania's President, Maaouya Ould Sid'Ahmed Taya, was in Saudi Arabia attending the King's funeral. While he was away, a group of renegade soldiers seized control of the country, announcing, "The armed forces and security forces have unanimously decided to put an end to the totalitarian practices of the deposed regime under which our people have suffered much over the last several years."

## Scott's Story

At the time of the coup, I was negotiating a petroleum concession with Taya's oil minister. When the coup leaders appointed a
new minister, my employer sent me there to meet with him.

Planes flying into combat zones follow a safety protocol.
My plane flew into Nouakchott under the cover of darkness. As
it approached from the Atlantic Ocean, it turned off all of its
lights, and we shut the window shades. The descent was steeper,
too, making it harder for anyone to shoot at the plane. My stomach felt the same way it did on a descending roller coaster. This
also made the landing faster and harder than usual. When the
plane halted, the pilot told us that the plane's right engine would
run while passengers disembarked on the left side—citing this as
"a requirement of its insurance company."

My security detail met me on the runway. There were two
vehicles, one of which was a lead that traveled a few blocks ahead.
Its responsibility was to survey the route for any signs of danger,
as occasional firefights continued in the streets. The lead vehicle
could then radio my driver to adjust course and avoid the gunfire.
But for the occasional patter of automatic rifles in the distance
and the hurried movements of young boys with large guns, most
citizens were continuing their day-to-day lives.

What I learned in Mauritania was that danger is easily avoid-
able, even in times of conflict. The fighting was not going on
everywhere, all the time. It was comprised of sporadic, little bat-
tles, here and there. Danger was very time and place specific. Life
went on, albeit more cautiously than usual.

Toward the end of my trip, I asked my bodyguard what was
the strangest thing he had seen in Nouakchott.

"The city of the dead," he said, without pausing.

"Is that a cemetery?" I asked.

"Yes and no," he said. "You see, there are thousands of Africans trying to immigrate to Europe. They come up from the south, and then they reach the Sahara Desert here. Mostly men, they often underestimated how much it would cost, and for many of them, Nouakchott becomes the end of the line. They are broke or nearly so, and there is no work to be found for them here."

"Can they turn around and go home?" I asked.

"Unfortunately, no," said my bodyguard. "They don't even have enough money to get back home."

I was beginning to understand the picture.

"You have to see it to believe it," he said. "I'll drive you there."

My bodyguard took me to the outskirts of the capital, where hundreds of West Africans were dispersed across an expanse of blowing sand. It was similar to a tent city, but the shelters were too flimsy to qualify as tents. We got out and walked along the edge of the encampment. Each resident had dug a hole in the soft sand, trying to find a way to cool down and escape the scorching Saharan sun. Most of them also had rigged a tattered shade over their hole in the ground, using what was left of their clothing.

A donkey cart pulled up beside me, carrying a big drum of water. Its driver jumped off and filled a bucket. After grabbing a ladle, he walked up and down the aisles of holes in the ground, selling drinks of water for a few coins to the few who still had enough left to afford one.

"The water comes from central storage facilities," said my bodyguard, "which are filthy. Nouakchott has hundreds of donkey carts like this one that collect and disperse water through the slums. *Médecins Sans Frontières* is currently fighting a cholera epidemic that is being spread by the water haulers.

"The men who get cholera are the lucky ones," he said. "They either die quickly, or maybe they get taken in and are fed by one of the hospitals or aid societies. The others are trapped. They don't have enough money to make it to Europe. Nor enough to go back home. When they can no longer buy food and water, they just die in their holes."

"What happens to their bodies?" I asked.

"A gravedigger from the city comes around. He deepens the dead man's hole and then buries him there. His home becomes his grave."

I looked across the masses but could not see any graves.

"Where are the buried?" I asked.

"The other side. These are the more recent arrivals. Newbies come camp here, gradually moving their little town further into the desert. The other side—closer to Nouakchott—is the cemetery. Like a sand dune, the refugee camp gradually crawls across the desert, leaving the dead and their refuse behind it."

My bodyguard then drove around to the back side. It was perhaps a hundred yards of rolling sand, with little sticks here and there, some of which had tatters of cloth attached to them, blowing like flags in the wind. Where the cemetery met the camp, the men were hardly moving. They were just waiting for the end.

The plight of refugees pulls on the heart strings. The lucky ones make it to Europe or the United States, where they seek asylum status. I wondered, though, whether the welcoming of refugees was an example of good-intentioned harm. Over the last decade, at least thirty thousand African refugees have died in transit. Even that number was based on published accounts of deaths, mostly sinking boats. They were not counting the ones whose journeys ended in unmarked graves. Would these people have lost their lives had Europe not enticed them to leave?

# 30. Bush Meat

*Cameroon*

AMERICAN EMBASSIES AROUND THE WORLD provide many wonderful services to citizens. The Gold Key package that the Embassies offer for purchase by American companies includes setting up meetings with local ministers responsible for overseeing investments and providing a local escort. The escort drives guests to meetings, explains customs, and serves as an interpreter, if needed.

One of the escorts at the American Embassy in Yaoundé, Cameroon, is a distinguished smaller gentleman. He is four and a half feet of unbridled enthusiasm. Rain or shine, he always greets you with a beaming smile. No matter how hot and sweltering the day, he dons a three-piece suit. With perfect English and manners fit for a Queen, he is a popular figure around the capital.

*Pangolin*

## Scott's Story

The Escort had worked hard all week, climbing many flights of stairs during periodic blackouts that turned government offices into saunas. On our last day in Cameroon, my colleague and I invited him to a fine dinner at "his favorite restaurant in Yaoundé." Those unfamiliar with Africa might think that fine dining in Yaoundé is an oxymoron. Yet almost every African capital has its share of elegant and expensive restaurants serving three- and four-figure French wines. Given the Escort's aristocratic appearance, that's what I was expecting when he picked us up at the Hilton.

Then we drove out of town, and the paved road gave way to red dirt. That's when I started to get concerned. The Escort's Mercedes expertly navigated the rutted road, eventually stopping at our destination.

"Welcome to the best restaurant in Yaoundé—the Dense Forest," the Escort said, his white teeth gleaming in the fading light.

A hand-painted sign read *Forêt Dense.* The establishment consisted of a small shack and picnic tables. Out back were several open fires. Shirtless Africans were roasting a variety of carcasses, turning the spits by hand.

The hostess welcomed the Escort, and they exchanged kisses on each cheek. She led us inside, which was simple but clean. It looked rather like a Texas bar-b-que joint. The Dense Forest was bustling, too. Most of the tables were occupied with smiling patrons. There were a few glances in our direction, but no one seemed surprised to see two Americans.

We ordered a round of cold beers and then took a look at the menu. While I do not speak French, I've spent enough time in French-speaking nations to navigate a menu. Yet none of the foods looked familiar. There was no *poulet* (chicken), no *boeuf* (beef), no *crevette* (shrimp). The only word I could make out was *serpent*—snake.

"What do you recommend?" I asked the Escort.

"Pangolin is the house specialty," he replied.

"What's that?" my colleague asked.

"It's like your armadillo," he explained.

I remembered seeing a National Geographic special on the endangered creature. I recalled that it lived in, well, the dense African forest. Then I realized where I was. It was a bush meat restaurant. Everything on the menu was a creature of the forest.

As the Escort walked us through the menu, the choices only got worse, culminating in various monkeys and bats. Basically, the fare was everything you might find crawling or flying around the rainforest.

When the waitress came to take our order, I asked about *poulet*. She said that could be arranged. My colleague concurred.

An hour later, the waitress brought the Escort's pangolin. It had been spit-roasted whole, and was being served on its back in a bowl of black gravy—with its four little feet and head pointing upward. When it was plopped on the table, it smelled awful.

The Escort wafted the aroma in the direction of his nose and closed his eyes in apparent ecstasy.

"Ah, the best smell in the world!" he exclaimed. "There's nothing like it."

At least I could agree with the "nothing like it" part.

The scene was surreal. Here was a man in a three-piece suit and tie making a bib out of his napkin so that he could feast on an endangered species. What followed next was a one-man feeding frenzy. The Escort dug into the pangolin's stomach and started plucking out its organs, swathing them with black gravy. He chewed on its scales. He plucked off its head and sucked on it.

All the while, the Escort was rolling his eyes and making guttural sounds of pleasure. He was enjoying the pangolin so much that I wondered whether I was missing something. My stomach actually grumbled as I tried to find meat on my own emaciated chicken. It seemed to be nothing but skin and bones. So, I ordered more beer and watched the Escort chomp away.

He plucked every bit of meat from every corner of the carcass until nothing was left but its empty shell and a pile of chewed up scales. The Escort's bib was filthy, splattered with pangolin and gravy. But the look on his face said it all. It was complete satisfaction. Could pangolin really be that amazing?

Back at the Hilton, we ordered a cheese pizza. Simple pizza never tasted so good.

*Kangaroo Island*

# 31. The Cat in the Hat

*Kangaroo Island*

Australia was a life sentence for the first European settlers. It was a far-flung prison for petty thieves of many kinds. Seven years was what they officially received, but no one could afford to return home afterwards. Servitude was a one-way ticket, and there was no going back. Perhaps it's not surprising that English settlers sought to remake Australia. They planted familiar trees and plants. And they brought their own English animals, releasing them into the wilderness. The native marsupials of Australia were no match. Rabbits and foxes multiplied and spread across the continent, forever changing its ecology.

The worst of these new residents was the house cat. The dwarf possums, bandicoots, bilbies, numbats, and other marsupials fell victim to it. As if tooth and claw were not enough, cats carried deadly European microbes in their feces, contaminating the soil and spreading death everywhere they trod. Feral cats have been blamed for 28 mammal extinctions in Australia. The aborigines—the oldest continuous culture on the planet—suffered greatly from the introduction of European animals. Fifty thousand years of living in harmony with the marsupial ecology evaporated in a few decades.

Contemporary Australia has awakened to the mistakes of the past. Australians seeking to restore the environment start small. They build enclosures in the wild and gradually expand cat-proof fencing to create sanctuaries for native wildlife. They also have taken to hunting cats.

Much of Australia's Kangaroo Island is a wildlife sanctuary. In addition to its namesake, it hosts such unusual creatures as the koala bear and platypus. Unfortunately, cats also have been gaining a foothold on the island. Leading the battle against them is the Kangaroo Island Cat Hunter. He's a tireless advocate for native marsupials and a sworn enemy of all invasive species—particularly cats. Our guide wanted to learn more, which led him to visit the Cat Hunter. He assured us that the Cat Hunter was the strangest thing he had ever seen.

## The Story of the Cat Hunter

"I knew I had reached the right place when I saw a sign that read 'Feral's End,' which had several cat carcasses hanging from it. The Cat Hunter came out to greet me. He's an older man, with a long white beard. Hanging around his neck were several cat pelts. He also was wearing a fur hat made from a cat pelt.

"The Cat Hunter explained that a single feral cat can kill thousands of native animals over the course of its life. He estimates that there are about 5,000 feral cats on Kangaroo Island and claims to have killed more a thousand of them on his nocturnal sojourns—putting a sizeable dent in their population.

"To fund his trapping costs, the Cat Hunter has turned his passion into a business. He skins his prey and uses their pelts for a variety of useful products. He showed me dozens of feral cat skins drying on a laundry rack.

"Next, he took me into his living room, which is a museum of his many products. His best-selling items are fur hats and shawls. His shawls come complete with two little cat paws that dangle from the ends. Cat skin trashcans are his third best seller. He also showed me cat pencil holders, bookmarks, and magnets.

"Since he mostly uses the furry pelts, he was left with a lot of cat heads. 'What do you do with a thousand cat heads?' he asked me. I shrugged. One of his walls has panels of curtains. The curtains were clearly made for a cat lover, as printed on them are pictures of cute kittens. Then he opened the curtains to reveal a wall of mounted cat heads, one on top of another and jammed ear-to-ear.

"'Modern art,' the Cat Hunter quipped. And then, 'What's in their mouths?' he asked.

"I approached and saw that several of their mouths had bird feathers in them.

"'The feathers represent the harm the cats do to the environment. You see, I'm a hands-on environmentalist.'"

As dark as the Cat Hunter's tale was, it has cultural significance. The earliest Australian settlers sought to remake Australia in the image of their lost England. Now, their descendants want to preserve what is left of the continent. The locals' passion for the Cat Hunter's products symbolizes Australia's new identity. Australians didn't have a revolution that severed their ties with England. Their cultural independence played out more gradually. The Cat Hunter's fight against his ancestors' invasive species is just a peculiar representation of Australia's evolving culture.

*Ebola Warning in West Africa*

# 32. Dr. Ebola

*Central Africa*

CENTRAL AFRICA IS A VERITABLE Garden of Eden. Its savannahs and forests are filled with an amazing diversity of creatures. In a matter of a few days, it's possible to see hundreds of bird species and three dozen different mammals in astounding numbers. Other equatorial paradises have their own array of species, but they all pale in comparison to the heart of Africa. World travelers sense that this place is special. Somehow, the circle of life has been spinning longer here than anywhere else on the planet.

The same is true for the smallest forms of life, viruses. The HIV virus originated around Lake Victoria. Residing nearby, too, are the viruses of the Filoviridae family. These are a family of viruses that cause hemorrhagic fevers—with very high fatality rates—in humans. Richard Preston tells the story of these viruses in *The Hot Zone*, describing how two Europeans contracted the Marburg virus while visiting Kenya's Kitum cave. The United States military descended on the cave, testing its creatures in search of the carrier, but came away empty-handed. The American government so feared that Filoviridae would be used as a weapon that it collected and stored the blood of survivors as an antidote just in case the virus was ever used to infect American leaders.

Marburg's close cousin, Ebola, ravaged West Africa in 2014, taking more than six thousand lives. Scientists believe that the entire outbreak originated when the virus jumped from a bat to a young boy, "patient zero." Patient zero and other children from the village frequented a hollow tree where a colony of tiny Angolan free-tailed bats lived. Hungry African children often catch these little bats and roast them over an open fire like marshmallows.

The Europeans at Kitum cave likely were infected by bats as well. Kitum cave is full of sharp crystals, which could easily have scratched or poked virus-infected bat droppings into the visitors—or perhaps the virus was lurking in the dust of the cave, which was then breathed in by the visitors as they hiked. Another theory is that bedbug-like parasites fed on bat blood and then bit the humans, transmitting the infected virus similar to the way mosquitoes transmit West Nile virus from birds to humans.

## Scott's Story

A decade before the 2014 Ebola outbreak made the virus front-page news around the world, I came within a few feet of it. I had just boarded a flight in Africa when a woman plopped a white Styrofoam container down on the seat next to me. I glanced at it, seeing that it was emblazoned with biohazard warning stickers. The woman proceeded to open the overhead bin and jam it in, next to my suitcase.

"I couldn't help but notice your baggage," I said. "What kind of biohazard is in there?"

"Have you ever heard of the Ebola virus?" she asked.

"Yes, I've read *The Hot Zone*. I also travel enough to Africa and South America that I subscribe to ProMED alerts, which provides business travelers like me with real-time updates on outbreaks and other health threats. I've seen a few alerts on Ebola. Is there live Ebola virus in your carry-on?" I asked.

"Not sure yet," she said. "I've just come from a suspected outbreak—sorry, but I can't tell you where. I'm rushing these blood samples from victims back to the Centers for Disease Control in Atlanta so they can be tested to confirm it's what we suspect."

"So, you're a doctor?"

"Yes, with the World Health Organization."

"Isn't it dangerous to carry onto a passenger plane the deadliest contagion in the world?" I asked.

"Yes, but it's less risky than checking it underneath the plane. Checked luggage is notoriously insecure here. Thieves may open and rifle through bags. Imagine if they did that to my blood samples. They could potentially infect themselves, with the results being catastrophic. Then there is the possibility of the container being compromised inadvertently—crushed by other cargo or dropped by a careless baggage handler. I can't let something so deadly out of my custody. Protocol demands that I personally carry the samples."

"Your little Styrofoam ice box did not look particularly secure," I said.

"To the contrary, it meets a triple packing standard. The sample is in a small watertight vial, which is then encased in absorbent packing material, which is in a watertight secondary canister. The virus isn't going anywhere easily."

"When you were there, was it as bad as the books make it sound?" I asked.

"Worse. Ebola basically melts the blood vessels. Blood then leaks out of internal organs and the eyes, ears, nose, and mouth, too."

"Why does the virus seem to come out of nowhere?"

"As you read in *The Hot Zone*, these viruses almost certainly have animal hosts that are not killed when infected. When the virus jumps to humans, it's almost too successful for its own survival."

As the 2014 Ebola epidemic raged, I thought of Dr. Ebola and how close I had come to the deadly virus—even if it were triple-packed. When scientists identified patient zero, they went to collect bats for testing. Unfortunately, the villagers had already burned down the bat tree. Even they suspected the bat colony was to blame. As the tree burned, the colony tried to escape. Many caught fire on their way out, and villagers described a "rain" of burning bat carcasses. Once again, the origin of the virus had eluded science.

# 33. One Person's Pet Is Another's . . . Dinner

*Ecuador*

QUITO, ECUADOR, IS ONE OF THE highest capital cities in the world, measuring in at nine thousand three hundred fifty feet. It's surrounded by even higher peaks. At nineteen thousand three hundred forty-seven feet, Cotopaxi volcano looms over the city, threatening it with rising columns of steam. Many thousands of residents live in Cotopaxi's evacuation zones, and the Ecuadorian army has stockpiled body bags in preparation for its next eruption. The iconic symbol of the city is a one hundred fifty-foot-tall statue of the *Virgen de Quito*. It depicts the Woman of the Apocalypse from the *Book of Revelation*, who fights a dragon—just as Quito may one day have to battle Cotopaxi. The vibe of a city can be hard to describe, but Quito's seems on the anxious side. Maybe that's because of Cotopaxi, and its menace of volcanic apocalypse.

*Guinea Pig for Dinner*

## Scott's Story

Guides and drivers come in all personalities. Our driver in Quito was a quirky young man named Andres. We immediately noticed that he compulsively twisted a lone curl of hair that hung down upon his forehead.

"Why are you twirling your hair?" Gina asked.

"It keeps me alert," he replied.

Yet Andres did not appear to have any challenges in that area. He talked fast and nonstop about whatever crossed his mind. Upon learning that we were Americans, he mentioned a recent trip to New York.

"What did you think of America?" I asked.

"I had issues with its lack of cleanliness."

I looked at Gina, and she at me. Then we looked out the window at the piles of trash lining the Quito highway.

"How so?" Gina asked.

"I was ordering a hot dog from a street vendor in Times Square, and he touched my bun with his bare hands."

"Do your street vendors touch the food?" I asked.

"Certainly not. I show you," he said, pulling off the highway and in front of a series of smoking stalls. "Watch," he said.

A man in the stall used a long fork to pluck a small carcass that was being roasted over an open fire. Then he placed the meal on wax paper, and artfully used the wax paper to wrap it. Andres was right. There was no finger-to-food contact.

"What are they eating?" Gina asked.

"*Cuy*. It's my favorite food!"

"What is that in English?" I asked.

"You call them guinea pigs."

"As in the big hamsters we keep as pets?" Gina cried.

"Yes," said Andres. "You can see them over there."

There were stacks of cages filled with live guinea pigs.

"I wonder what they must be thinking as they nervously stare at the flames," said Andres. "Sometimes I feel like a guinea pig too. I look out at Cotopaxi volcano smoking like the *cuy* do at the hibachi. Maybe we both share the same fate. Would you like to try some *cuy*?"

"I'm a vegetarian," Gina immediately offered.

"I could never be a vegetarian," Andres said. "My second favorite food also is meat. Have you heard of *Yawarlukru*?"

"What?" Gina asked.

"It's a stew of lamb intestines, livers, lungs, and blood."

In comparison, roasted pets sounded quite appealing. I'd take *cuy* any day over *Yawarlukru*.

"What is your least favorite food?" Gina asked.

"Chicken," Andres said.

"But everyone likes chicken," Gina said.

"Who doesn't like chicken?" I added.

"I grew up on a farm," Andres said. "We had lots of chickens. One day, my grandmother was decapitating a chicken when it escaped her grip. The headless bird flew right into my arms, flapping and covering me with its blood. To this day, I remain terrified of all chickens, whether living or dead."

"Have you ever heard the expression topsy-turvy?" I asked.

"Explain the meaning," Andres said.

"It means that someone is the opposite of what another considers to be common. To us, your food is topsy-turvy. You eat American pets and fear American food."

Andres laughed. "That's true of Ecuador and America, more generally. Americans pay a lot for organic food, and McDonald's is one of the cheapest restaurants. It's the opposite in Quito. Organic food is abundant and cheap while McDonald's is one of the most expensive restaurants. I take my wife to McDonald's for

Valentine's Day dinner. It's our most expensive meal of the year. The rest of the time we eat organic for a fraction of the cost."

After Andres dropped us off at our hotel on Plaza de San Francisco, I opened our window and watched the colorful promenade below. A homeless man carrying a trash bag caught my eye. He walked into the middle of the square and crouched down. Then he threw bird seed all around his feet. Like many plazas, it was home to large flocks of pigeons. Hundreds of them immediately came, surrounding him. I had seen this before from pigeon-lovers in Venice, New York, and elsewhere.

But this man had other plans. He swung his arms into the mass of pecking pigeons, capturing a dozen of them. With a violent squeezing, he crushed them against his chest. When the last of them stopped moving, he plopped the dead birds into his bag. The other pigeons didn't even notice. They continued to eat at his feet. The pigeon hunter then walked off across the square, swinging his bag and whistling a happy tune.

*Abu Dhabi Mosque*

# 34. Be Careful What You Admire

*Emirate of Abu Dhabi*

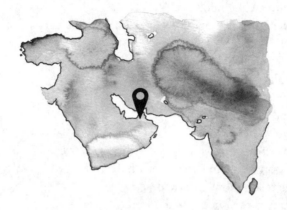

Abu Dhabi is the richest of the seven United Arab Emirates, producing more than two million barrels of oil per day. One of its traditions is the making of extravagant gifts. The classified section of Abu Dhabi newspapers even offers a column called "Unwanted Gifts," in which recipients of jewelry and exotic vehicles anonymously convert them into cash. A closely related tradition is the *obligatory* gift. If you openly admire another's possession, then the owner must give it to you.

## Scott's Story

I lived in Abu Dhabi for a year, working closely with the royal family on a natural gas project. On my first visit to the Sheikh's palace, I was offered dates from the palace gardens. I had never been a fan of dates, but these were particularly delicious. I complimented them openly, and as it turned out, praised them a little too much.

That evening I was working in my apartment when there was a knock on the door. I was not expecting any guests so it caught me by surprise. When I looked through the peephole, I recognized the apartment's bellman.

"Delivery," he said.

I opened the door, and he had a luggage cart piled six feet high with boxes.

"You must have the wrong apartment," I said. "I haven't ordered anything."

"The palace has sent these."

"Sent what?" I asked.

"Dates," he replied.

I was speechless as he unloaded box after box.

As soon as he finished, he said, "I'll be right back."

"There are more?" I asked.

"Many more," he replied.

Over the course of the next hour, the bellman ferried cart after cart of dates. By the time he was finished, there was hardly space to walk in my small living room. The dates' sweet smell was so overpowering that I found it difficult to sleep. The next day, I had them shipped to the office, where they were distributed to co-workers by the crate.

The dates were just the beginning of the gifts, though. As the business relationship grew, so did their grandeur. When a visiting vice president complimented the in-seat air conditioning of the palace car sent to retrieve him, an identical new one was delivered to him from the Mercedes dealership, complete with the in-seat air conditioning. The company policy forbade such gifts, but local custom made it offensive to return them to the Sheikh. So the Mercedes was confiscated by the company—where it ended up being used to run errands around town.

In both cases, the Sheikh was expressing the Arabian tradition of *karam* or generosity. Arab traditions arose in the hostile environment of the desert, and the kindness of strangers was often necessary for survival. The host today may be the desperate visitor tomorrow.

I have heard three different explanations for the practice of obligatory gifts. The first is that compliments of things indicate envy or jealousy—the guest wishes he or she also possessed the item. To alleviate these feelings and make the visitor feel more comfortable, the host gives the guest whatever was being admired. This brings the visitor up to the level of the host and makes everyone feel more comfortable together.

The second account is that most Arabs believe that God is always at work, controlling everyone's destiny. When a guest admires something, God is speaking to the owner. Maybe this is God's way of saying that the host values the item too much and should demonstrate his or her faith by relinquishing it.

Lastly, Arabic culture is indirect. People do not usually come out and ask for things, no matter how badly they need them. It's a tradition for arriving guests to be offered tea. No matter how thirsty they are, they decline the initial offer. The host offers a second time. The visitors decline again. Only on the third time will the guests accept. This can create comic scenes in souks when shopping westerners keep rejecting the offer of tea, and the host just thinks they are being excessively polite—so the offers keep coming again and again. The same principle may be at work with obligatory gifts. Hosts may interpret the compliments as indirect requests for the items.

*Gabonese Soldiers*

# 35. The Red Carpet Isn't For Me

*Gabon*

WE HAVE MET MANY DIGNITARIES in our world travels. While executives can be schooled in protocol, some naturally have the right diplomatic instincts—and others, well, don't. One thing we've learned is that it's always better to err on the side of deference than risk offending someone. This is doubly true when visiting the Republic of Gabon.

The Republic of Gabon is a small nation on Africa's Atlantic coast, bisected by the equator. Inland, its dense jungles are home to gorillas and forest elephants. But the coast is rich with oil. For forty-two years—from 1967 until his death in 2009—Gabon was ruled by Omar Bongo, making him the sixth-longest-serving (non-royal) ruler in the history of nations, joining such illustrious company as Cuba's Fidel Castro and North Korea's Kim Il-sung, at fifty-two and forty-eight years in power, respectively. Bongo's longevity was largely attributed to his shrewd deployment of the nation's oil wealth. "What's the fastest way to become rich in Gabon?" one resident asked. "Start an opposition party." Bongo was more likely to buy off his rivals than have them killed, coopting them rather than alienating them. His presidential palace was rumored to have cost $800 million, and he made his way around the nation on his personal helicopter.

## Scott's Story

I traveled to Gabon in 2006 to discuss the prospect of an oil deal with Bongo's administration. I was invited to the presidential palace to meet with the President's daughter, who was Bongo's chief of staff. Joining me on the trip was another oil executive from Houston.

Libreville is a steamy equatorial city and prone to downpours. A thunderstorm had just passed over the capital. Its torrential rains had flooded the usual approach to the palace, requiring us to enter the grounds through the rear gate. The guards there instructed us to walk across an expansive lawn to reach it.

The palace's yard also served as Bongo's helicopter landing pad. The President's big white chopper was sitting smack in the middle of the lawn. Running from its steps all the way to the palace's back door was a gorgeous red carpet.

It was 100 degrees out and 100 percent humidity, and we were hiking across the grounds in our suits. The wet grass was soaking through our shoes and pant legs. As we passed the helicopter, my colleague made a beeline for the red carpet. I opted to continue forward on the grass. My instinct told me that the carpet probably was not meant for two Americans, however wet our shoes might be.

Upon reaching the red carpet, my colleague waved to me, smiling, and looking smug and proud. His smile didn't last long, though. In a matter of seconds, I heard yelling from behind us. Two presidential guards with guns drawn were shouting in French and running toward my colleague. He saw them, too, and then looked down upon the red carpet. Realizing his mistake, he quickly stepped off of it and back into the grass.

I quickened my pace, walking on through the wet grass to the palace, confident that the guards had no issue with me and wanting to avoid the altercation. When I reached the palace door, I stopped and waited for my colleague. The guards were still pointing their machine guns at him, and his hands were in the air. I wondered whether they were going to arrest him, but they ended up letting him go. He then walked rapidly across the lawn to join me, so embarrassed that his blushing face was as red and bright as the carpet he had tried to walk on.

*Our Askari*

# 36. The *Askari*

## *Tanzania*

NORTHERN TANZANIA IS A LANDSCAPE of soaring volcanoes and the yawning craters they left behind. Millions of tourists take game drives through the largest of these, Ngorongoro Crater. The area's second largest crater—Empakai—is rarely visited. The winding, bumpy road to Empakai eventually ends on its rim, which offers two spectacular views. In one direction is Oldonyo Lengai, a steaming, active volcano about 10 miles to the north. Into the crater itself is Lake Empakai, a thousand feet below. Unlike Ngorongoro, there is no road to the Empakai floor. The only way to reach it is by hiking down forested slopes along steep and slippery trails.

Empakai's forest is home to two of Africa's most dangerous animals—the leopard and the Cape buffalo—neither of which should be encountered on foot while unarmed. When we embarked on our hike into the Empakai crater, we needed an *askari*—one who walks in your shadow as a protector. Our *askari* led us into the crater, his assault rifle always at the ready. The trail was barely wide enough for one person, with sheer cliffs rising or falling on one or both sides.

"More buffalo use these trails than people," said the *askari*. Fortunately, we encountered only birds and bugs on this day. When we reached the crater floor, there was a large troop of baboons playing along the lakeshore. The *askari* pointed to fresh tracks in the mud. "A leopard just passed by," he said. "He is hunting for a baboon."

Scott asked the *askari* when was the last time he had to fire his gun.

## The Askari's Story

"Just a few weeks earlier, I was walking on a trail similar to this one at Ngorongoro Crater. Coming right at me was a Cape buffalo. There was no place for either of us to get out of the other's way. It could not turn around, and the beast charged. I fired, killing it with a single shot.

"I had expected that the falling buffalo would tumble over the cliff. Instead, its momentum carried it forward, sliding in my direction. It finally came to rest only a few steps in front of where I stood. Its carcass was so large that it blocked the entire trail.

"I consulted with my group, explaining that they could either climb over the buffalo carcass and continue—or turn back. The family opted to continue on their hike. One by one, I helped each to climb over the smelly beast.

"About an hour later, we returned on the same trail. Only, when we reached the buffalo, two lionesses were perched on its back, eating it. We stopped, and I readied my gun. First, I shouted at the lionesses. They glanced up, and then went back to eating.

"Then I fired a shot into the air, trying to scare them away. One of the lionesses snarled back at me, baring her teeth. Three more lionesses from the other side of the trail joined the feast.

"The park does not allow an animal's life to be taken unless it is a clear and present danger to a person. The Cape buffalo had been charging at us. It was okay to shoot it. But these lions were merely enjoying their meal. It was we who were in their way. Moreover, there were too many lions. It would have been impossible to defend us from them all. So, we had to turn around and take another trail, the long way around the lions."

*Arctic Polar Bear*

# 37. The Polar Bear

*Arctic Ocean*

Barrow, Alaska, is the northernmost point in the United States, sitting on the icy shores of the Arctic Ocean. Temperatures drop below freezing in early October and stay there until late May. For as many as one hundred sixty of these days, temperatures will stay below 0 degrees F. Not only are Barrow's winters cold, but they're also extraordinarily dark. The sun sets in mid-winter and doesn't rise again for more than two months.

## Scott's Story

I often visited Alaska while working for the Trans-Alaska Pipeline, which transports crude oil from the Arctic across Alaska to the Pacific port of Valdez. On one of my trips, I hired a polar bear guide in Barrow. His trip consisted of two parts—we would tour by dogsled in the morning and then, in the afternoon, we would explore the Arctic using a special truck with tank tracks.

When we arrived at the dogsled location, the sled dogs were all sleeping on top of their doghouses, their fur covered in white frost.

"Why are the dogs not inside?" I asked.

"By Barrow standards," he replied, "this is a mild morning, only -4 degrees F. That's too hot for the dogs to sleep inside."

While the dogs were being roused from their slumbers and hooked up to the sled, I asked my guide the question.

"What's the strangest thing you've ever seen up here?"

"I survived a plane crash," he replied.

"Go on," I said, urging him to continue.

"It was a small company plane, with a forward luggage compartment in its nose and two props on its wings. As the plane took off, the nose compartment came open, spilling its contents. These struck one of the engines and the wing. In a matter of seconds, the plane was out of control. There was never a chance for bracing. We crash-landed onto sea ice in the Arctic.

"As the plane bounced and slid, I was aware of it all. It felt like an eternity before the plane finally stopped. I tried to move from my seat, but the pain in my back was excruciating. I wasn't paralyzed, but I had broken my back. Miraculously, everyone survived. The pilots were concerned that the plane might catch on fire, or break through the ice, so we all had to go outside, into the frigid air. As we waited for rescuers, things got worse. A polar bear showed up and began to circle us. The captain shot off a couple of flares, but the bear just ignored them. It continued to circle closer until a coast guard helicopter arrived on the scene. Only then did the beast run off."

"What are the odds that we will see a polar bear today?" I asked.

"Very good. They've been coming in to feed on a whale carcass."

Before we got in our sled, my guide gave me a brief course in dog sledding. In addition to "Mush," which, of course, means let's go, I was introduced to the fundamental commands of "Gee" (right turn) and "Haw" (left turn). He also showed me where the holster was, pulling out a large stainless-steel revolver.

"Do you know how to shoot one of these?" he asked.

"I've been shooting all my life," I replied.

"This is a .44 magnum. Although it looks flat on the tundra, the ground rises and falls. We may not see the bear until we are on top of it. If we surprise one, I may use the gun to haze it and scare it away. It's loaded with five rounds of blanks."

"What about the sixth round?" I asked, recalling that most revolvers I had previously shot held six bullets.

"The sixth is a regular bullet," he said.

"Is one round enough to kill a polar bear?" I asked.

"That one's not for the bear. It's for me."

That morning, there was no need for drawing any weapons or scaring anything, as the largest creature we saw was an Arctic fox.

After lunch, we headed farther out of town in a truck with tank tracks. Several miles up the beach, the locals had left the remains of a whale killed in a recent hunt. As we approached the whale carcass, I saw my first polar bear.

"There's one!" my guide shouted.

Only instead of being white, it was yellowish.

"Why's it yellow?" I asked.

"Some of the bears get algae in their coats that turns them yellow. It's not unusual this time of the year."

As we approached, the polar bear bolted for the sea ice, disappearing behind an iceberg in the distance.

We then drove around the whale carcass to confirm that there were no more bears hiding in or around it, and my guide invited me to get out and have a look. He pointed out where the bear had been eating, and estimated its size based on its paw prints in the snow. Farther on we spotted fresh tracks from two polar bears, the yellow one that we had just seen and another, much larger one.

"That's a monster," my guide said. "Look at how much larger its tracks are. Let's see if we can find it. We are about to walk out onto the sea ice. Beneath us is the Arctic Ocean. The spring thaw is underway, and the ice field is breaking up, like a giant puzzle, leaving cracks of varying sizes between its pieces. Those gaps can sometimes be hidden by fresh snow. If you step on the snow, you'll fall straight down into the ocean. There will be nothing I can do to save you. To prevent that from happening, I'm going to walk ahead, and you follow me, stepping exactly in my footprints."

"Exactly in your footprints," I repeated.

My guide marched out onto the sea ice, following the fresh polar bear tracks. Step by step, I carefully matched his footfalls. We had been moving for about ten minutes when he stopped and pointed at the icy ground.

"Watch this," he said, kicking at the snow.

Six inches of snow fell straight down a crack into the ocean. I could see the water sloshing around about two feet down.

"That's what I was talking about. The blowing snow can hide the seams."

From there on, the puzzle pieces of ice became smaller and some of them shifted with our weight. After another twenty minutes of hopping over crevices, we approached a jumble of low icebergs, perhaps ten yards by ten yards in diameter. I could see the polar bear tracks going into them but not coming out.

My guide stopped and walked backwards to me. "The bear is in there," he whispered. He was out of breath and looked scared. "I want you to walk back to the truck as fast as you can, stepping in our footprints. Keep going and don't look back—no matter what happens."

Turning, I could see the truck in the distance, but it seemed very far away. I was surprised at how far on the ice we had ventured. We were certainly more than a mile out. I turned and started heading back, much faster than before. I moved quickly from one piece of ice to the next, some of them wobbling and shifting under my weight. I occasionally glanced over my shoulder, and my guide was right behind me.

When we were back in the truck, he apologized for getting us dangerously close to a polar bear.

*Tsetse Fly*

# 38. Tsetse Fly Food

*Serengeti Plains*

THE TSETSE FLY USES ITS LONG proboscis to pierce through multiple layers of clothing to feed on human blood. It also is the carrier of a deadly parasite: African trypanosomiasis, or sleeping sickness. Under a microscope, these tiny creatures resemble eels. Once inside a mammal, the parasites rapidly reproduce. While human infections number only a few thousand each year, the tsetse devastates Africa's livestock, causing losses of $4 billion annually.

In Moses's time, the fourth plague of Egypt was likely tsetse flies: "If you do not let my people go, I will send swarms of flies upon you and your officials, on your people and into your houses." The fifth plague was a disease that wiped out the Egyptians' livestock. Could this have been African sleeping sickness?

While sleeping sickness kills cattle, African animals possess a natural resistance to it. Whenever agriculture tried to establish itself where tsetse flies lived, European livestock (and some-times the people, as well) perished. Consequently, the geographies of Africa's national parks substantially correlate with areas of tsetse infestation. Without tsetse flies and the parasites they carry, much of Africa's natural wonder may have been lost. It also means that tsetse flies may be among the wildlife encountered by park visitors.

## Gina's Story

We took our entire family on a three-week trip across East Africa, culminating in a tented safari in Serengeti National Park in the midst of the Great Migration. The best estimates of the migration are that it encompasses about two million wildebeest, half a million gazelle, and a quarter of a million zebra—almost three million large mammals in total. We spent a fortune to be placed in the midst of this spectacle. Only when we arrived, the plains were empty and quiet. Where were the animals?

While the wildebeest should have already reached our camp, their migration had been disrupted by "unseasonable rains." The wildebeest were missing—but the tsetse flies were swarming in anticipation of their arrival. Maybe they were even angrier than normal, furious that their food was running late. Our family's arrival was the next best thing. We were effectively serving ourselves up as a tsetse fly appetizer.

Prior to this trip, we had been all over Africa and had rarely even seen a tsetse fly, much less been bitten by one. How can we be so sure? Because you definitely know when a tsetse fly bites you. The pain is sharp and shocking, rather like an immunization needle. None of us had ever felt anything quite like it.

As soon as the open Land Rover stopped, the tsetse flies were upon us. They were undeterred by our insect repellent. Khaki clothing also was supposed to help, but it made no difference whatsoever. Khaki pants or blue pants, the flies landed and bit. We responded with layers of clothing and scarves wrapped tightly around our necks and faces. Still the flies would land and probe, and wiggle their way under the garments—until they found a spot where their long pokers could suck our blood.

The only effective deterrent was physical vigilance. Our guides gave each of us a severed cow tail tied to the end of a stick. No further instructions were required. We waved and swatted whenever the swarms descended. If the flies could not land, they could not bite.

Being back at the camp was no better. Dinner was served outside, under the stars and gas lanterns. The tsetse flies may have been asleep by then, but thousands of other insects had just hatched from the unusual rains. By the time waiters placed our first course of pumpkin soup in front of us, its surface was covered with drowning winged bugs. The flickering lanterns on our table only attracted more of them. They turned the white tablecloths into a veritable horror movie, sending us running for the safety of our zippered tents.

After a day of this misery, we instructed our guide to drive us to the Great Migration—even though it was four hours away. The long drive was definitely worth it. The scale of the migration was so large that it cannot be adequately captured by a camera, or even the eyes. There are just so many animals. They moved across the plain in long, snaking lines that stretched from one end of the horizon to the other. Upon meeting a river crossing, the herds would pause, piling up on each other and growing in numbers, until the earliest arrivals were pushed into the river by the latecomers. Then they would spill rapidly across the water, swimming as fast as they could through gauntlets of hungry crocodiles. It was an awe-inspiring experience—and fortunately, without any flies, since they were happy to feed on the wildebeests.

African tourists are not routinely devoured by tsetse flies so I researched whether we should be worried about sleeping sickness. The International Association for Medical Assistance to Travelers states that "[c]ases of sleeping sickness continue to be reported in tourists, many have been in or near Serengeti." Newspaper articles also describe sporadic cases of travelers returning from Serengeti National Park with sleeping sickness. Nonetheless, I was reassured to learn that the probability of contracting the disease was remote because only a small percentage of the flies actually carry the parasite.

We all returned home healthy, filled with memories of our participation in the Serengeti's circle of life. We were more than observers. We had been, well—tsetse fly food.

# 39. The Concierge

*South Australia*

ADELAIDE IS THE CAPITAL of South Australia. Its principal claim to fame is that it was *not* founded as a prison colony. Whereas Sydney and Melbourne were born as prisoners' settlements, Adelaide's settlers came there freely, mostly as farmers. They started off trying to grow wheat and other staples, but the surrounding valleys turned out to be perfect for a much more valuable crop.

## Gina's Story

We traveled to Adelaide for the same reason most Americans do—to taste the greatest Shiraz wine in the world. An hour north of Adelaide is the Barossa Valley, and an hour south, the McLaren Vale. These valleys have unique soils, full of obscure minerals that convey depth and complexity to the region's wines. Some of the rocks in which the vines grow are more than one billion years old. The mix of cool winds from the Southern

*Downtown Adelaide*

Ocean and hot, dry winds from the Outback incubate the grapes to perfection.

Late one evening, we were having dessert at our hotel, when the concierge caught our eye. The young man was sitting behind a desk, validating parking and generally looking bored. We decided he might enjoy some interesting conversation. We walked up to him and announced ourselves as writers working on a travel memoir.

"Surely," I said, "a concierge sees many unusual things here. What's the strangest request you've had from a visitor?"

The concierge blushed and stuttered.

"I'm a professional and must respect guest privacy."

"We aren't looking for names," I said. "You can leave those out."

"I can't think of a story," said the concierge.

He looked genuinely stumped.

"We'll give you a day to come up with one," I said. "Expect us back tomorrow. You better have a story by then!"

The next day was our last in Australia. We were at the R.M. Williams store in downtown Adelaide trying on boots. Unfortunately, the downtown store did not have our sizes, but a suburban one did. We hailed a cab and raced across traffic trying to make it to the store before its 5:30 p.m. closing time. When it was clear we would be late, Scott called the manager there and persuaded her to keep her doors open after closing time.

It was a testament to how nice Australians are. They even have a name for it—"mateness." Mateness must have come from the need of people to be helpful in such a sparsely populated, hostile environment. And we were happy to be the beneficiaries of mateness that evening.

The store manager greeted us at the front door with a smile. She also introduced us to her daughter, who had come over to keep mom company. What would have been a hurried transaction anywhere else in the world turned into a leisurely evening. We tried on different shoes while the manager and her daughter got to know us. When we mentioned the name of our hotel, the manager beamed with pride, asking whether we might have met her son.

"He's the concierge there," she said.

It turned out that he was the one and the same concierge we had interrogated the evening before.

"Your son has promised to tell us a story about the strangest thing he ever saw at the hotel," I said.

"Ask him about the famous Australian actress who greeted him at the door in lingerie and tried to have her way with him," recommended the sister. "When he rejected her advances and fled down the hall, she screamed after him, 'Don't you know who I am?'"

"My son was once a celebrity himself," said the mom. "He was the host of Australia's #1 children's show."

She reached into her purse and handed us a CD of the show's greatest hits.

"You can keep it," she said. "I'm so proud of him."

Before leaving the store, we made both mom and sister promise they would not let the concierge know about our meeting until tomorrow. We wanted to have some fun with him.

Later that night, we approached the concierge again at his desk.

"Remember us?" I asked.

He turned red.

"Well," I said, "I've heard a story about you."

"I knew there was something more to this," he said. "Is there a camera somewhere?" The concierge leaned across his desk, searching for a camera.

"Do you recognize her?" Scott asked, pointing to me.

"You do look familiar," the concierge acknowledged. "Have I seen you on television?"

"While she is not as famous as some of your guests," said Scott, "she's friends with an actress."

"Oh, no," said the concierge.

"In fact," I said, "my friend, the famous actress, stayed here once before."

The concierge blushed even redder. "I didn't do anything with her," he proclaimed, clearly recalling the incident.

With that, I pulled the CD out of my purse and held it up, referring to the concierge by his stage name. This attracted the attention of his colleague. He walked over and grabbed the CD from my hand.

"Is that really you?" his colleague asked.

"You must be working with my producer," the concierge said. "He put you up to this, didn't he?"

At this point, I confessed it was his mom and sister who were responsible. We recounted the "It's a Small World" moment of how we had all met in suburban Adelaide earlier that day.

"All right, you've earned your story," the concierge said. "I was working the night shift, and around 3 a.m., an older business-man came into the lobby accompanied by two buxom ladies. Not a block away from here is Adelaide's version of a red-light dis-trict—Hentley Street—which is frequented by prostitutes. The businessman appeared to have found a couple of them. As the elevator doors closed, he drunkenly shouted, 'It's my lucky night!'

"I was concerned by the appearance of the two prostitutes. They were tall, and their hands and feet were masculine. I hoped the businessman was getting what he expected. A few minutes later—too short for any business to have transpired—the two prostitutes exited the elevator without their client and hurried out into the night.

"I chuckled, wondering what had happened upstairs. Not five minutes later, the businessman stumbled off the elevator in his underwear. He ran outside and looked both ways down the street. 'They're gone, aren't they!' he cried.

"I took him into an office and tried to calm him down. He had been robbed. I offered to call the police, but the embarrassed businessman declined."

# 40. Valley of the Mole Rats

*The Rift Valley*

AFRICAN MOLE RATS ARE NOT PRETTY. They're small, hairless mammals possessing four long incisor teeth (two on the top and two on the bottom), which are used for digging tunnels and defending the colony. What they lack in beauty, they make up for in good health. Mole rats are immune to cancer, which helps to make them the longest living rodents—up to thirty years. Consequently, they have been the subject of considerable medical research.

The mole rat also is the only mammal known to live in eusociality. Think of bees, ants, termites, and wasps. Eusociality means that there is a sexual division of labor among the hive's members, with a queen at the apex of the organization, a handful of breeding males, and the rest being workers (which do not participate in reproduction). Mole rat colonies have a similar organization. Only one female and a few males reproduce, and

*African Mole Rat*

the rest of the mole rats support them as workers. The smaller workers dig tunnels, gather food, and maintain the nest while the larger ones are soldiers responsible for defending the colony in case of attack.

A single colony's territory may extend the length of several football fields, with the winding tunnels serving various purposes. Some tunnels access tubers, which provide the mole rats with both food and water. Mole rats also have surface holes for purposes of foraging on grasses. Other rooms include a nursery where the queen rears her young, pantries where food is stored, and toilet chambers. Mole rats are preyed upon by birds (when they come to the surface) and snakes, which enter their tunnels. Upon sight of a predator inside the tunnels, an alarm is sounded, and the soldiers use their long incisors to attack the snake while piling upon themselves tightly to effectively "plug" the tunnel and prevent the predator from going any deeper.

## Scott's Story

We were driving on a bumpy dirt road through the highlands of the Rift Valley, near the Tanzania-Kenya border. There were no trees, just unending vistas of grass-covered hills. We came over a rise and looked down on a verdant valley that extended for miles before us. Only something was different about this view.

The grassland was punctuated with small dirt mounds every ten yards or so. At a distance, this made the landscape look speckled.

"What causes the mounds?" I asked.

"Mole rats," our guide said. "There!" he shouted, pointing to one as it scurried across the road in front of us. "And another," as a mole rat crossed in the other direction. They were everywhere, running back and forth across the road, and ducking in and out of their holes.

"Do you see the birds of prey circling?" our guide asked.

Across the valley, there were dozens of hawks and eagles, circling and swooping.

"They are feeding on the foraging mole rats," our guide said. "Each of the little mounds is an entrance for a colony. The rats run out into the grass, find something to eat, and then hurry back. Most make it back home, but some don't."

As we drove across the Valley of the Mole Rats, I watched this bird-and-mouse game play out. They had a brilliant system. There were so many tunnel entrances/exits that it enabled the massive colony to forage its entire territory while never being (too) far from safety. The most amazing aspect of these animals was how many there must have been. We descended into the valley and drove for several miles. The whole way, there were mole rats in every direction, as far as the eye could see. There must have been millions of them.

# 41. The Real Equator

*Ecuador*

ECUADOR IS LOCATED, AS THE NAME IMPLIES, on the equator. Its capital city, Quito, lies only fifteen miles south of the equator. To take advantage of its proximity, the Ecuadorians built a grand monument called the *Mitad del Mundo*—"Middle of the World." It's a tall column topped with a giant globe. Running right up to the monument is a big stripe marking what is supposed to be the equator itself. Only their measurements were wrong. The actual equator lies a few hundred feet away, on private land.

We had several hours in Quito between arriving from the Galápagos Islands and catching our flight back to the States. We hired a driver to see something, anything, other than the airport. We asked him to take us to the strangest thing he had ever seen in Quito. Our driver said that the strangest thing he had seen is kept behind locked doors at the Museo Solar—the museum built by the private landowners on the real equator. Unfortunately, night had fallen, and the museum was closed.

*The Real Equator?*

## Gina's Story

"What are the highlights of the museum?" I asked.

"I cannot tell you. You must see it for yourself," said our driver. "Maybe on your next trip."

"Surely, there is someone who could open the museum for us?" Scott asked.

"Will you pay extra?"

"Certainly," Scott said.

I jabbed Scott in the ribs and whispered in his ear, "How much extra would that be? You need to get the price first."

Our driver made two calls, and then turned back to us.

"It is possible," he said. "One hundred dollars."

"Agreed," Scott said.

"This mystery better be good," I said.

Half an hour later, we pulled off the road and parked in a dusty ravine. It was dark, and there was no sign of a museum. Dogs were barking furiously nearby. This did not look at all safe.

"We're here," said our driver. "The museum's at the top of the trail."

We followed closely behind him, arriving at the museum's entrance. The gate was closed and locked with a chain and padlock. Everything was dark, and there was no one in sight.

"They are coming," he said. "Now we wait."

I looked around. There was a sign that said $4 for admission.

"See the sign," I said, pointing it out to Scott. "This is their lucky night."

We saw a flashlight from the other side of the entrance gate.

"He's here," said our driver.

"Welcome to the equator," said the young man holding the flashlight. He took out his keys and opened up the gate for us. "This way," he said, as he flipped a circuit breaker that lit up the hillside. There were various thatch huts connected by trails.

The guide led us to a patch of concrete with a red line painted down the middle of it.

"That's the real equator," he said. "The one at the *Mitad del Mundo* is wrong. They didn't have GPS forty years ago when they built it."

"How do we know this is the true equator?" Scott challenged.

"I will show you," the guide said, dragging over a gold sink and putting its drain exactly over the red line and setting an empty bucket beneath it.

"In the northern hemisphere, the curvature of the Earth causes water to drain in a counterclockwise motion. In the southern hemisphere, it's clockwise. But on the equator, water drains straight down. Here, I will show you."

The guide threw a handful of leaves into the water and pulled the plug. Sure enough, the water ran straight out the drain without any discernible rotation.

"Look! Look!" he said, excitedly.

The guide then moved his golden sink ten feet to the north and poured a bucket of water into it. This time, the water appeared to drain in a counterclockwise motion as he had predicted.

Then he dragged the sink ten feet to the south of the line and repeated his trick. The water was now draining in a clockwise motion.

It turns out that the Coriolis effect demonstration really is a parlor trick. Still water pours straight down, and the rotational effects are triggered by how the guide pours the water into the sink.

Scott walked over to our driver. "Did I really just pay $100 for this? Is it really the strangest thing you have ever seen here?"

"No. That's not it. Later, my friend. Later."

The guide continued with his equator tricks. We had to walk on the red line, trying to keep our balance—which admittedly seemed more difficult than ten feet to either side of it. I also was given an egg and told to balance it on the head of a small nail positioned exactly on the equator. It was not as easy as the guide said it would be, but I eventually got it to stand on the nail head.

The driver and guide then started speaking in Spanish. Their conversation was quite animated, but the guide finally appeared to agree with the driver. They led us up the hill to a room containing the owner's collection of curiosities—stuffed Amazonian animals, birds, and tribal weapons. Among the collection was a shrunken head.

The guide brought it over and placed it on a table in front of us. "Do you think this is real?" he asked.

"No," I replied.

"You're right," said the driver. "That's the fake one. It's the one all of the tour groups are told is real. It's all they ever see."

The guide then opened a locked cabinet and brought out a much older looking specimen. "This is the real shrunken head," he said.

The shrunken head was only the size of a clenched fist but clearly showed the delicate features of a young man.

"This head came from the Shuar tribe, in the foothills of the Andes," he explained. "The Shuar believed that the head-shrinking process captured the spirit of their victim within the shrunken head, thereby protecting the killer from otherworldly revenge."

Scott tried to take a photo, but the guide grabbed his iPhone. "No photos of this one."

"How did they make it so small?" I asked.

"After chopping off the victim's head, the Shuar would carefully peel the skin from the skull, starting at the back of the head—to better protect the victim's facial features. The skin would then be boiled in an herbal solution for about an hour. After boiling, the removed skin was filled with sand or pebbles and placed in the sun to shrink. When the shrinking process ended, a wooden ball about the size of a fist was inserted inside."

"Is the mouth sewn shut?" asked Scott.

"Yes! The shrunken head's mouth and eyes were sewn shut, which also is believed to secure the victim's spirit."

The little head with its tiny features was one of the creepiest things that we've ever seen. It's no surprise that travelers to Ecuador in the 19th century prized shrunken heads as souvenirs. They were the highlight of many a Victorian library's curiosity section. The demand became so great that curio shops in Quito offered a gold coin for each shrunken head. This led to an unfortunate consequence—headhunting parties. The Shuar would set out on murderous conquests to satisfy tourists' taste for the morbid. It wasn't until the 20th century that Ecuador finally banned the trade in shrunken heads.

The last known headhunting expedition took place in 1961. A group of European tourists was passing through the Ecuadorian Amazon when they came across a headhunting party. The warriors were returning with the freshly severed heads of their victims and proudly displayed the trophies. One of the party even filmed part of the resulting ceremony. It's the only known video footage of head-shrinking.

On the way back to the airport, we debated cultural preservation. While it is sad to see the world's differences disappearing, there are some cultural practices that are best left behind. Headhunting, we agreed, is certainly one of them.

# 42. The Land of Hospitality

*Japan*

BUSHIDO, OR "THE WAY OF THE WARRIOR," governed the lives of Japanese nobility for centuries. Its principles included strict loyalty, honor, and politeness. The samurai warriors may be long gone, but their spirit still survives in Japanese corporate life. This is particularly true of the Japanese *keiretsu*—a form of Japanese business organization in which a group of companies each owns some portion of every other member company. The interconnectedness of the members fosters a mutual stability.

## Scott's Story

I had the opportunity to spend several weeks in Japan, negotiating with one of the largest *keiretsu*, which traced its roots back to the 17th century. Every meeting with the *keiretsu* embodied careful ceremony. When business cards were exchanged, the recipient

*Samuri Reenactment*

received the card with both hands, bowed slightly, and then held the card high and close to the face until it had been carefully read. Business cards were exchanged in a strict order, starting with the most senior person in the room. Once received, they were treated with careful respect. They could not be written upon or placed in a cardholder. Typical American practices of haphazardly flinging cards across a conference room table, or worse, forgetting someone's card after a meeting, would cause offense.

Seating also followed ancient rituals. Guests were not allowed to sit just anywhere around the table. The highest-ranking visitor would occupy the "seat of honor," or *kamiza*. In conference rooms, the *kamiza* is typically the seat farthest from the entry door. This is sometimes also referred to as the "safest" position. In Bushido times, attackers (ninja or samurai) would come through the entrance. The person in the safest position could then be more easily protected.

On one of my trips, I was joined by a very large American lawyer who was both tall and heavy. Sumo wrestlers excepted, most Japanese are of smaller and lighter stature than a typical American. My hosts placed me in the *kamiza* and my lawyer in the adjacent seat, only slightly closer to the doorway. The only problem was that the conference room chairs were on the smaller side. When my lawyer sat down, his chair collapsed under his weight, sending him to the floor. My Japanese hosts were mortified. They helped the lawyer to his feet among a rain of apologies.

Then the meeting was postponed. Everyone was escorted out of the building to a café. We were served drinks for about an hour before we were allowed to return to the conference room. Upon arriving, I immediately noticed a change. The small chairs had been replaced in their entirety by the largest, most comfortable chairs I had ever seen.

I visited Japan several more times for meetings at the *keiretsu*, and always enjoyed the luxury of big chairs.

*Vodun Ceremony*

# 43. The Home of Vodun

*Togo*

Tourists to New Orleans may encounter "Voodoo," a mixture of religious beliefs brought to Louisiana by West African slaves. American Voodoo has been heavily commercialized for tourism. There are Voodoo museums, midnight tours, and visits to the graves of Voodoo kings and queens. Tourists can even buy Voodoo dolls with pins, presumably to lay curses on their own enemies. Across the Atlantic Ocean, though, in the heartland of West Africa, the real religion survives. It's called "Vodun."

## Scott's Story

Vodun are spirits that co-inhabit both nature and society. The creator of the world in which we live—and of these spirits—is Mawu, a female god. She often is paired with a masculine counterpart, and their children are imbued with various powers and charged with overseeing different domains. Animals and trees may be empowered by the Vodun spirits. This is why animal parts are sold in West African markets as charms.

In the West African Republic of Togo, there are more than two million practitioners of Vodun. I ventured several hours into central Togo to meet with one of its tribal kings. While our focus was on business, the King invited me to join him at an important Vodun ceremony taking place in a nearby village.

My driver followed the King's entourage over bumpy, red dirt roads with gaping potholes. Only a four-wheel-drive could have made it here. As we approached the village, there were people, mostly dressed in white, walking in from every direction. When the crowds blocked the road, the King pulled over and parked, and we did the same.

As soon as my door opened, I could hear—feel, even—the rhythmic drums pounding in the distance. The King walked up to me holding a two-foot-long golden mace.

"You will be the only outsider here," said the King, "so you must stay close to me." Then he paused. "For your own safety."

We were far north of Togo's capital and an hour from the nearest paved road. I was probably the only non-Togolese for a hundred miles in any direction. I never left his side.

"The purpose of this ceremony is to bless the village," said the King, as we walked together toward the pounding drums. He held his mighty gold mace before him, and the crowd parted for us.

"This is where we stop," he said. "No closer."

The vantage point was a good one, though. Before me, I could see dozens of drummers behind a large tree, beating their haunting rhythm. Several hundred villagers, all dressed in white robes, followed each other in a single-file line, which spiraled around the tree and into the adjacent fields. The altar, so to speak, was at the base of the tree. There was a pile of animal heads stacked there, alongside of which solemnly stood a man and woman.

"Those are the high priestess and priest," the King said.

The priestess was particularly striking. Like the others, she was dressed in a white robe. She wore a white headdress atop her head, and dozens of long beads hung down her neck. Her face was painted with white spots. The priest wore a white skirt, but was shirtless with beads wrapped around him.

A man carrying a goat led the procession. The goat was calm, not struggling at all. Immediately behind him were a dozen topless women with their naked bosoms painted white.

"Watch the priest," the King said.

The priest lifted a long, curved dagger above his head and then swung it across the goat's neck, opening its carotid artery. Even with the blow, the goat was silent in its holder's arms. The next woman in the procession held a large wooden bowl beneath the goat, catching the river of its blood.

As the goat died, the electricity in the crowd grew, and the drums beat louder and faster. The procession advanced, with each person dipping his or her fingers into the bowl and then rubbing the goat's blood across their mouths. Most showed little reaction, but a few of the topless women started spinning in a wild frenzy. One's eyes were all white, rolled back into her head.

A woman near me grabbed my arm and started yelling at me in her local language. She was clearly angry. She turned to the crowd and shouted, pointing at me.

"It's time for you to leave," the King said. "It will not be safe for you to watch anymore."

With that, the King's people hurried me back to my car. There's no general prohibition of non-practitioners attending these ceremonies, and tourists routinely watch Vodun animal sacrifices in West Africa without incident. What was different about this one?

While rare, there are reports of human sacrifice continuing in West Africa. As recently as 2007, Reuters described six killings that occurred over the course of one weekend in Togo: "The discovery of the headless corpses has shocked Togolese and triggered a wave of speculation that the killings were ritual murders. This is a practice still found in parts of Africa in which people kill to obtain body parts and blood in the belief they will bring social success and political power."

# 44. The Hidden People

*Iceland*

ICELAND IS A MOST UNUSUAL PIECE of geography. It sits atop the Mid-Atlantic ridge, straddling both the North American and European continental plates. The dividing line between those continents is abundantly visible as it cuts across the landscape—a gradually widening, deepening ditch. It's this unusual position that causes Iceland's frequent volcanic eruptions. In 2010, the Eyjafjallajökull volcano spewed so much ash into the atmosphere that it closed air traffic across much of Europe for a week. On the more benign side, tourists enjoy swimming in the island's many hot springs and marveling at geysers spraying.

While Iceland, befitting its name, certainly has a lot of ice due to its location near the Arctic Circle, its south coast benefits from the warmth of the Gulf Stream. Vikings settled Iceland in 874 AD—more than seven centuries before the English arrived in Virginia. At first, the Vikings thought they were the first to

*Glacier Hiking in Iceland*

arrive, having discovered a new and uninhabited land. It turned out they were not alone.

## The Old Farmer's Story

"I grew up sixty years ago on Iceland's east coast. Back then it was even less populated than it is now. We lived almost entirely off the land and had little contact with anyone else.

"One of my earliest memories is my parents warning me about the Hidden People. The story goes that when the Earth was a paradise, its first family—Adam and Eve—had a large family. One day, Adam was fishing in the river when God said that he would be visiting his house later that day to check on him and Eve and see how things were going. Adam ran home as fast as he could and told Eve the news. Eve was concerned because she was not being a good housekeeper or mother. The house was messy, and her children were dirty. She frantically picked up and started bathing the children. Before she could finish their baths, she heard God approaching. She took her dirty children and hid them in a closet.

"'Oh, Eve,' said God, 'your home is so tidy. Let me see your children.'

"Eve paraded her clean children before God.

"'And your children are so clean, too.' Then he paused. 'But are these all of your children?' he asked.

"Eve continued her lies, and God became angry. 'What you hide from God shall be hidden from you and all of your descendants.'

"When Eve returned to the closet, the dirty children were missing. She could hear them crying for their mother. 'Why can't you see me? Here, mommy.' Even though Adam and Eve never saw them again, they still left food for them—which always disappeared. Adam and Eve also cautioned their other children never to throw rocks—for fear they might strike and injure one of their hidden siblings.

"So, I grew up believing that other human beings—that we could not see—lived among us. We would put food outside for them at Christmas, and it was always gone. While the Hidden People are normally invisible to us, we sometimes catch glimpses of them."

"Have you ever seen one yourself?" asked Gina.

"Yes, many years ago, on our farm. The weather was colder then, too. Fogs would roll in, so thick you had to know the land perfectly to avoid getting lost. You might only be able to see what was at your feet. My parents warned us that God would lift his punishment during fogs—since it was impossible to see them. They could come out of the caves where they live and wander freely. Every fog, something would change. A tool would disappear. A tree might be cut down, leaving only a stump. A lamb might go missing and never be found.

"When the fog would come, we would hurry around to secure everything we had—against the Hidden People. Several times as I was doing so, I would hear a rustle, and see one running away from me. So, yes, I believe in the Hidden People because I have seen them with my own eyes."

"What about younger people—are the beliefs changing with technology?" Gina asked.

"There was a survey in which only a small percentage of us— mostly older people like me—still believe in the Hidden People. But when the surveyor asked whether they would build their home on a location where Hidden People were once seen, 97 percent of them said definitely not. They would build elsewhere."

When the Vikings arrived in the 800s, there were Gaelic monks already secretly living there in Iceland's caves. The Irish historian Dicuil wrote in 825 AD of "many other islands" in the north Atlantic and that "one reaches them from the northerly islands of Britain, by sailing directly for two days and two nights with a full sail in a favorable wind the whole time . . . and for nearly a hundred years hermits lived there, coming from our land, Ireland, by boat." Archaeological evidence from caves along Iceland's south coast and the Faroe Islands to the south appear to substantiate the presence of hermits. They presumably left civilization to get away from people and likely sought to avoid their Viking neighbors (no surprise there).

Perhaps it was Iceland's original hermit cave-dwellers who gave rise to the captivating legend of the Hidden People. Maybe they were inadvertently sighted from time to time. The hermits might have snuck into Viking settlements to steal food and other tools. Fog would have provided them with a convenient cover. The hermits also probably did not take care of their appearance. Maybe they were dirty and unkempt—just like Adam and Eve's hidden children.

*Hanoi's Sea of Scooters*

# 45. Sea of Scooters

*Vietnam*

HANOI, VIETNAM, HAS A POPULATION of seven million people—and three and a half million scooters. Two, three, four, or more people pile on to each scooter, clinging to each other, and they crowd the roads. Yet they all move forward—albeit slowly—toward their destinations. This mass of scooters was our dominant first impression of Hanoi, and our most enduring memory of the city.

## Gina's Story

On our first night in Hanoi, we had dinner at the Metropole Hotel's street side café in the old French Quarter. We were sitting on a busy corner, watching the spectacle of jam-packed scooters making their way without the assistance of any traffic light. The speed was slow enough that the cyclists could work in or out of the flow as needed. Crossing the street looked absolutely impossible, although locals managed easily. They would wade right into the traffic and, miraculously, safely emerge on the other side of the street.

Our itinerary for that evening had us walking alone to the Water Puppet Theater, a short distance away, and then meeting a local guide to take us on a tour through Hanoi's night markets. Getting to the Water Puppet Theater, however, would require us to cross the sea of scooters that we had been marveling at over dinner. We stood on the corner for several minutes waiting for a gap in the traffic. When we finally saw one, we hurried quickly into the street, only to have the gap disappear before our eyes. We now found ourselves smack in the middle of the street. We were trapped, frozen, and unable to move forward or backward. Yet no one honked. The scooters just drove around us as if we were a light pole.

Patience paid off, however. Gaps eventually presented themselves, and we slowly advanced forward, step by cautious step. Eventually we made it to the other side. We were relieved.

The remainder of the walk to the Water Puppet Theater was on pedestrian streets entirely closed to traffic, and when the show was over, our local guide was waiting for us.

"We will be crossing many streets on our walk," he said. "The first thing you need to learn is how to cross like a local."

We related our difficulty in crossing the street next to the Metropole, and he laughed loudly. "Last week," he said, "I was supposed to meet a couple of Americans at the lake. Fifteen minutes passed. Then half an hour. They were really late. I knew they were staying at the Metropole so I decided to go check on them. As I approached the hotel, I saw them standing on the corner of the street. They would take a step or two out into the traffic and then retreat back. By the time I reached them, they had been trying, unsuccessfully, to cross one street for almost an hour.

"Follow me," he said, leading us to our first street crossing. It looked even worse than the Metropole. It was a wall of scooters, with no discernible gaps.

"First," he explained, "you must look in the direction of oncoming traffic and walk slowly and steadily into it. Once you are in the midst of the scooters, you continue to walk at the same pace all the way across the street—and this is most important—without stopping or pausing or hurrying. In doing so, the scooter drivers anticipate your course and easily steer around you."

I was skeptical of how this would work.

"Watch," our guide said. "I'm going to walk first to illustrate. You follow behind me at the same pace, and do exactly as I do."

Sure enough, he walked right into the crowded street, and the scooters adeptly avoided him. Scott and I did the same. The scooters simply moved out of our way. They came close to bumping us but never did.

The first few times I crossed, it felt awkward and uncomfortable, but then I got the hang of it. By the end of our tour, I was looking for streets to cross, and enjoying the power of being a pedestrian in Hanoi.

*Australian Road Kill*

# 46. Road Kill Art

*Australia*

WHEN WE WERE TRAVELING THROUGH AUSTRALIA, we often saw kangaroos, snakes, and other wildlife dead along the roadways. One of the saddest scenes we came across was a stretch of roadway on which thousands of potatoes had spilled out of a farmer's truck. Kangaroos and wallabies had descended on the roadway to gorge themselves on the lost produce. Unfortunately, many of these marsupials had met their demise in the process. One poor wallaby, lying twisted and bloody on the side of the road, still held within its mouth a half-eaten potato. Its last meal. The scene led our guide to tell us about his encounter with the Road Kill Artist.

## The Road Kill Artist's Story

"As you can see from the carnage," our guide said, "marsupials and automobiles are not a good combination.

"I had an unusual request from a guest who wanted to be picked up at 11 p.m. to go wildlife-spotting. Sure, it was on the late side, but I agreed to take him.

"Only when I met him, he had a whole luggage rack of art supplies. There were multiple canvases in different sizes and lots of paints and brushes.

"'What's all this for?' I asked.

"'I'm going to paint road kill. Your job is to help me find road kill, and we are going to stop at every one.'

"I imagined that we would stop on the road, with the headlights on the massacred animal while he painted the poor, deceased creature. Only that's not at all how this went down.

"Every time we saw an animal, we stopped. While I waited in the car, the Road Kill Artist would walk up to the dead creature and closely examine it. He would get down on all fours on the road and crawl around the animal, tilting his head and considering it from different angles. The first dozen or so that we saw, he rejected, telling me to simply drive on.

"Then we finally found one that was good enough for him. It was a wallaby flattened in a particularly twisted way. He took a big brush and proceeded to slather the creature's fur with brightly colored paints. Blues. Greens. Reds. As soon as he was satisfied with the color scheme, he took one of his canvases and pressed it onto the roadkill. When he lifted it up, he held it up in the headlights, showing off his handiwork. The animal, like a woodcut, left its colorful impression behind on the canvas, including the texture of fur. While his tactics were strange, the result was not unattractive. I would have paid good money for the artwork.

"We drove through the countryside like this for the next couple of hours until he had exhausted his canvases. On the way back to the hotel, he passed me $100 and swore me to secrecy.

"'You're an accomplice to a crime!' he said, which was news to me. 'The Australian Wildlife Act makes it a crime to exploit wildlife, whether dead or alive. You have just broken the law!'

"I asked him what his favorite road kill painting was, and he showed me a photo of a kangaroo baby—a joey—painting on his iPhone. The little guy was done all in various shades of blue.

"'How did you get that one?' I asked him, wondering how a joey managed to end up separated from its mother's pouch.

"'We were going down the highway in the middle of the night when the kangaroo hopped into the middle of the road and froze in our headlights. As we came to a screeching stop, the mother reached into her pouch, pulled out her joey and threw it right into our windshield. Then she bounded off as fast as she could.

"'When we checked on the joey, we found it was already dead. Whether it had died from the impact or the realization that its mother loved herself more than it, who knows.'

"Now, that's survival in the Outback—a mother sacrificing her baby as a diversion so that she can escape."

*Cape Buffalo*

# 47. Don't Mess with the Cape Buffalo

*Malawi*

THE CAPE BUFFALO IS ONE OF Africa's five most dangerous animals, or "Big Five." It stands almost as high as a man at its shoulders and weighs upwards of two thousand pounds. Hunting guides refer to the Cape buffalo as the "widow maker," a name it has earned by killing two hundred humans each year.

We were with our guide in Klein's Reserve, a valley that runs between Kenya's Maasai Mara and the Serengeti. Large herds use Klein's Reserve to migrate between the two national parks. The valley floor was packed with one thousand Cape buffalo feeding on the tall, green grass. While we were watching, the herd became spooked. The animals ran off in one direction, stopped, and then ran in the other direction.

Our guide panned the horizon with his binoculars until he found the cause. A pair of lions were mating nearby. Shifting winds were carrying their scent in different directions. While the lions had better things to do than hunt, the buffalo could smell the predators but were unsure of their location.

We asked our guide, Massey, whether he had any good buffalo stories.

## Massey's Story

"I grew up in a village in Malawi. Each day, my friend and I would walk more than five miles to elementary school, and it was common for us to encounter wildlife along the way. Cape buffalo were of particular concern, and we had been taught what to do if we encountered one. While the buffalo is impossible to outrun in a straight line, it is slower than a human when it has to run in a circle. Thus, if a human can run around a termite mound or tree, it's possible to outrun the buffalo (which hopefully will eventually tire and move on).

"When we were on our way to school, we came across a large male buffalo standing in the middle of a muddy lakebed. We froze, preparing for it to charge at us. Yet the buffalo just stood there, motionless. Then we realized it was stuck in the mud. My friend tossed a stone in its direction to see whether it could move. The buffalo snorted and turned its head, but was indeed stuck.

"We started throwing one small rock after another at the great buffalo, trying to hit its horns. With each throw, the buffalo grew angrier, snorting ever louder. We could see its muscles rippling under its hide, as the mighty creature rocked back and forth in the mud. Then my stone found its mark, making a loud noise as it struck the bridge of the buffalo's horns.

"That did it. The angry buffalo pulled free and started to climb out of the muddy lake, heading straight for us.

"I looked behind me, but it was too far to run for a tree. Our only option was to run around the lake.

"Once the buffalo reached the shore, it gave chase. As our elders had advised, humans were faster at running in a circle, and we managed to keep ahead of the beast. Unfortunately, the part about the buffalo tiring was not coming true. Perhaps the others had not been taunted with rocks.

"After several minutes of running, we were slowing. The Cape buffalo was starting to gain on us, getting a little closer each time we circled the lake. I shouted to my friend that we should run into the middle of the lake before it catches us. I cleverly thought that the mud would better support our lighter weight, and if the buffalo followed, it would sink and get stuck again.

"So, we bolted toward the muddy waters and made it to the middle, where we instantly sank up to our thighs. Like the buffalo before us, we were completely stuck in the mud. The more we moved, the higher the mud advanced. It was like quicksand.

"The buffalo made a start like it was going to come in after us, but then it stopped and just watched, occasionally snorting.

"As we waited for a charge, I remembered the second lesson from my father. The buffalo kills with its horns, which curve upwards. If a buffalo is about to get you, lie as flat as possible to the ground, and it will be unable to hook you. Buffalo know this, too, and they have a trick to make people get up. They will lick a person's ears. This licking has caused people to lift their heads, only to be immediately gored.

"Yet the buffalo did not come onto the mud. It seemed satisfied that the tables had been turned. Its tormentors now were suffering its old fate. After making a few faux charges, it left us there, trapped in the mud. It was not until much later in the day that a passerby finally pulled us to safety."

*Tanzanite Miner*

# 48. The Tanzanite Miner

*Mount Kilimanjaro*

Tanzanite is a blue-violet gemstone that occurs in only one location in the world—the Merelani Hills near Africa's highest peak, Mount Kilimanjaro. The stone was discovered on the surface of the hills in 1967 by an amateur prospector. He was unable to identify it, so he sent samples to New York. Why did it take so long to find this gemstone? The answer appears to be a 1960s-era fire. Heat tends to bring out the vivid blue-violet colors, and a wildfire had raged through the area, making the crystals in the hillside come alive and glow. But for the accident of the fire, we might not have tanzanite today.

While the name may seem obvious (Tanzania = tanzanite), it was coined by the jeweler Tiffany & Company. Enamored with its blue beauty, Tiffany's christened the gem "tanzanite" as a marketing tool to emphasize its exotic rarity. Tiffany's proclaimed that it could only be found in two places: Tanzania and Tiffany's.

Almost fifty years later, tanzanite is still found only within a five-square-mile area. It's never been mined elsewhere in Africa, or for that matter, the world.

This sliver of East Africa is geologically special. It's part of the Great Rift Valley, where the African continent is being ripped apart by plate tectonics. Here, the rocks have succumbed to incredible metamorphic forces, spawning extraordinary minerals like tanzanite. We came across a former tanzanite miner, who told us the true story of how the gemstone is mined. It may make you think twice the next time you see one.

## The Tanzanite Miner's Story

"The owner paid for our room and board, and the dynamite needed to blast mine shafts. In exchange, we contributed our labor. The owner, who did not mine himself, got 50 percent of any discovery, and the other 50 percent was divided among all of the miners equally.

"We started our mine at the surface, blasting a vertical shaft one stick of dynamite at a time. After each *boom!*, we went into the hole and hauled out the rocks. As the hole became deeper, we built makeshift wooden ladders, which we used to go deeper and deeper until we were about a hundred meters down. This became our access shaft.

"At the bottom of the access shaft, we built a second, horizontal tunnel. The tunnel was not even tall enough to crawl on all fours. We slithered on our bellies, like worms. When we met another miner going in the opposite direction, our sweat-soaked bodies struggled to slide past each other.

"Yet the tunnel grew every day, as we chipped away, sending rock back up to the surface for examination. We chased veins of fool's gold, which can lead to tanzanite. All of our hammering created a fine dust, which we inhaled, making it even harder to breathe in the cramped quarters. I still have nightmares of the dust choking me in the blackness of the mine.

"Remember, there were no wages, only room and board. The equal division of the miners' 50 percent was made no matter how long each miner had been working. If there were ten miners, a $1,000 payout was divided equally among them in ten $100 shares—even if one of them had only been working one day and the others for many months. Miners came and went, and it wasn't fair that someone who had dug for a year would share equally with someone who happened to arrive on a lucky day.

"After two years, though," he said, and then tears welled up in his eyes and ran down his cheeks, "no tanzanite had been found in our mine. We were all ruined men, left with nothing to show for two years of hard labor. I quit the business and trained to become a safari guide.

"Not long after my departure, sudden torrential rains hit the Merelani Hills. The tanzanite mines are open, vertical shafts, and the runoff flowed into them like drain pipes. The miners were hundreds of meters down and had no idea what was happening. There was no way they could be warned. The flood waters roared into the narrow shafts, drowning many of them, including two who had worked alongside me. Had I discovered tanzanite, I might have still been there. I too might have drowned with my friends."

*Elephant in Ngorongoro Crater*

# 49. The Elephant Graveyard

*Ngorongoro Crater*

AFRICAN ELEPHANTS LIVE LONGER than sixty years. Like humans, older elephants have dental problems. Elephants start life with as many as six sets of teeth. As each set wears down over years of eating, the next one slides in to replace it. Eventually, though, the last molars grind down to the gums. When that happens, the elephant must find softer food. They have no choice but to change their diets. Marshes have an abundance of soft plants, and this is where old elephants often spend their last years.

Tanzania's Ngorongoro Crater shelters Ngoitokitok Spring, which creates a perpetual marsh. This is the perfect environment for old tuskers, and they come here to finish their days. Tusks of the oldest males can be enormous, almost ten feet long. This elephant retirement home (and burial ground) is also one of the best picnic locations in the Crater. We enjoyed a memorable breakfast at Ngoitokitok Spring. Then our guide pulled out a ball, and he and our kids played soccer on the crater floor as zebras ran in the distance.

After the game was over, he told us the most interesting thing he had ever seen at the spring.

## The Guide's Story

"Not far from here, there was a bull elephant lying on its side. I thought he was dead but wanted to make sure. I kept my guests at a safe distance and walked over to investigate. First, I touched its back. There was no response.

"Then I kicked one of its legs. Still no movement. As a last measure, I knelt down by its mouth to check for breathing. All was quiet.

"Now that I was confident that the elephant was dead, I called everyone over and allowed them to feel the skin and lift up its heavy trunk.

"Everyone was gathered around the elephant when suddenly its gut moved and a guttural sound came from inside its mouth.

"I was terrified and yelled, 'Get away!'

"I was sure the elephant was alive and about to get up and charge us.

"Before we could run, though, a blood-soaked hyena emerged from the elephant's posterior. The hyena saw the crowd of onlookers, panicked, and then bolted right through their midst.

"Even I screamed as it ran by me. In an instant, the hyena was gone. Then we all laughed about it.

"That was the last time I ever approached a dead animal on foot."

# 50. Mayan God

*Guatemala*

GUATEMALA'S LAKE ATITLAN IS REGARDED AS one of the most beautiful lakes in the world. The views across its thousand-foot-deep waters and towering volcanoes alone would be sufficient enticement for travelers. But most people come here for something else—to visit the villages lining its shore. Here, the ancient culture of the Mayans has managed to survive the onslaught of technology—at least for now.

## Gina's Story

We chartered a boat from our hotel, Hotel Casa Palopó, and ventured out across the lake. The villages line the lake, each rising steeply up the volcanic slopes. Over the course of the day, we hopped among them by boat. While they all shared the general

*Dinner at Hotel Casa Palopó*

Mayan culture, each specialized in different arts and crafts. As we walked through the narrow streets, I asked our guide what was the strangest thing he had seen on the lake.

"Maximón," he replied, "is a Mayan idol in Santiago de Atitlan. He is moved annually from house to house. The hosts effectively turn part of their home into a religious shrine. All day long, Maximón is guarded by volunteer caretakers who allow access to the idol. Parishioners and shamans arrive daily, waiting for their turn to undertake various offerings and rituals."

"Is Maximón a good god?" Scott asked.

"Neither good nor evil. He is viewed as a balancer. Maximón represents a link between the Mayan underworld and heaven. Thus, his worshippers may petition him for healing—but they also may ask him for curses and revenge."

After we arrived in Santiago de Atitlan, our guide took us on a winding hike to try to visit Maximón's shrine. The last several blocks were like a maze; we had to walk single-file through nearly vertical alleys filled with dogs. The final alley dead-ended into a home where there were a dozen Mayans sitting on the cobblestones.

"The shrine is in that house," our guide said. "Those people are waiting to worship Maximón."

"Is it okay for us to visit?" I asked.

"For the right price," our guide said, smiling and holding out his hand.

Scott got the message and passed him several bills.

"Wait here," said our guide, as he stepped over the waiting Mayans and into the house. He emerged about five minutes later.

"Follow me," he said, leading us past the line. "The last worshipper just finished. A new ceremony is about to start." He moved us to the side of the room and against the wall. "Over here. That is Maximón."

Maximón was a short idol composed of a mannequin head topped with a big cowboy hat and draped with dozens of scarves and ties. At Maximón's feet were various bowls and offering dishes filled with money, flowers, and bottles of liquor.

The room itself was still and dark, lit only by candles—and completely filled with choking smoke. My eyes burned, and I felt like I couldn't breathe. Every bystander was smoking. Cigarettes. Cigars. Even Maximón had a smoldering cigarette stuck into his prosthetic mouth. The fog was so thick that the air seemed to glow orange.

We watched as an old man led a young woman into the room. They knelt before Maximón. The woman then lit a cigar, puffing on it to get it going, and then exchanged it for Maximón's cigarette.

"The old man is a shaman," whispered our guide, "and the woman has hired him to help her win Maximón's favor."

The shaman started chanting and placing various offerings from the woman in the bowls, including a bottle of liquor. Then the woman started crying. She was clearly in great pain.

Our guide leaned over and whispered, "She wants Maximón to intercede and make her man love her again."

It was a sad ceremony in more ways than one. Here was a poor woman, who was spending what little money she had to pay a shaman and buy cigars and liquor for an idol. While she may have had some psychological relief, her investment otherwise seemed wasted.

The nearby Mayan highlands were at the center of Guatemala's civil war, which killed as many as 200,000 people over four decades. The resistance sometimes used Maximón as their symbol. The war may be over, but many of the guerrillas kept their weapons and organized into gangs. These gangs now terrorize the region and profit from drug trafficking and other organized crime.

That night, we were eating dinner on the balcony of our hotel, with the moon reflecting off Lake Atitlan below us. As our waiter was pouring me a glass of wine, the popping of gunshots echoed up the hillside, immediately followed by yelling. The waiter did not even react.

"Did you hear that?" I asked.

"Hear what?" he responded.

Had the hotel trained him to pretend the violence outside its gates didn't exist, or was he so used to hearing it that he now tuned it out?

# Acknowledgments

⌒

"What's the strangest thing you've ever seen or experienced?" It was the people who answered our question that made this book possible. So first and foremost, we wish to thank everyone who shared their incredible stories with us.

Over the course of our travels, we took notes on several hundred stories. Then we needed the right team to help us compile them. So we researched and read the best travel writing we could find. One name kept appearing—Don George. We also recognized his smiling face from our *National Geographic* catalogs, where he led immersive journeys of like-minded travelers. We are so grateful for Don agreeing to work alongside us. He helped us select these fifty stories from so many others and then challenged us to make them the best they could be.

Don also assisted us in crafting a book proposal that caught the attention of Larry Habegger at *Travelers' Tales* publishing of Palo Alto. We would like to thank Larry and his team of editors and designers for realizing our vision for *Strange Tales of World Travel* and enabling us to finally share these stories with readers around the world.

We hope that this book will inspire other travelers to ask questions like ours and truly experience the strange world we live in.

# About the Authors

Gina and Scott Gaille grew up in small towns in central Michigan and south Texas. Even then, both dreamed about exploring the farthest corners of the planet. Gina's favorite TV show was *Hart to Hart*, whose globetrotting detectives—played by Robert Wagner and Stefanie Powers—journeyed to South America, China, and Australia. Scott spent Sunday evenings glued to *Mutual of Omaha's Wild Kingdom*, whose safari-jacketed host, Marlin Perkins, introduced him to exotic landscapes and their peoples. Gina is most passionate about Africa, where she once served as a missionary in a remote part of Kenya. Scott's career as a lawyer and academic at The University of Chicago and Rice University has taken him to more than 100 nations around the world, including 30 in Africa. It was their shared passion for experiencing the world that brought them together.